D0577736

CODY HIGH SCHOOL
Dist. No. 6
CODY, WYOMING

NO. IV 4

The Yale Shakespeare.

◄◄◄◄◄◄◄◄◄◄◄◄◄◄◄◄◄◄◄◄◄►►►►►►►►►►►►►►►►►►►►►

THE TRAGEDY OF KING LEAR

NEW EDITION REVISED BY

TUCKER BROOKE

PUBLISHED ON THE FUND
GIVEN TO THE YALE UNIVERSITY PRESS IN 1917
BY THE MEMBERS OF THE
KINGSLEY TRUST ASSOCIATION
(SCROLL AND KEY SOCIETY OF YALE COLLEGE)
TO COMMEMORATE THE SEVENTY-FIFTH ANNIVERSARY
OF THE FOUNDING OF THE SOCIETY

This new edition of KING LEAR and a number of other plays in THE YALE SHAKESPEARE has been prepared by TUCKER BROOKE who has used, added to, and brought up to date the work of the previous editors whose names appear with his in the separate volumes.

The Tragedy of
King Lear

EDITED BY TUCKER BROOKE

AND

WILLIAM LYON PHELPS

New Haven · Yale University Press

LONDON · GEOFFREY CUMBERLEGE

OXFORD UNIVERSITY PRESS

Copyright, 1917, 1947, by Yale University Press

Printed in the United States of America

NEW EDITION

Second printing, August, 1952

Third printing, January, 1955

Fourth printing, March, 1956

All rights reserved in the editorial contributions to this
edition, which may not be reprinted, in whole or in
part, except by written permission of the publishers.

CONTENTS

The facsimile opposite represents the title-page of the Harvard copy of the First Quarto of 'King Lear.' Bibliographers now agree that the Second Quarto, though purporting to have been issued in the same year, was actually printed in 1619. Of the genuine edition of 1608 twelve copies and of the other thirty-two are known to survive. The two editions do not vary in the descriptive part of the title-page, except in spelling and press-work, but the falsely dated one has a different printer's device and imprint, as reproduced below from the Elizabethan Club copy.

Printed for *Nathaniel Butter.*
1608.

M. William Shak-speare:

HIS
True Chronicle Historie of the life and death of King LEAR and his three Daughters.

With the vnfortunate life of Edgar, *sonne* and heire to the Earle of Gloster, and his sullen and assumed humor of TOM of Bedlam:

As it was played before the Kings Maiestie at Whitehall vpon S. Stephans *night in Christmas Hollidayes.*

By his Maiesties seruants playing vsually at the Gloabe on the Bancke-side.

LONDON,
Printed for *Nathaniel Butter*, and are to be sold at his shop in *Paules* Church-yard at the signe of the Pide Bull neere St. *Austins* Gate. 1608.

[THE ACTORS' NAMES

LEAR, King of Britain
KING OF FRANCE
DUKE OF BURGUNDY
DUKE OF ALBANY
DUKE OF CORNWALL
EARL OF KENT
EARL OF GLOUCESTER
EDGAR, Son to Gloucester
EDMUND, Bastard Son to Gloucester
Lear's Fool
CURAN, Servant to Gloucester
OSWALD, Steward to Goneril
Old Man, Tenant to Gloucester
Doctor
A Captain, in Edmund's service
A Gentleman, Attendant on Cordelia
A Herald
Servants to Cornwall
GONERIL,
REGAN, } Daughters to Lear
CORDELIA,
Knights of Lear's Train, Officers, Messengers, Soldiers,
    and Attendants

SCENE: Prehistoric Britain.]

The Tragedy of King Lear

ACT FIRST

SCENE FIRST

[King Lear's Palace, Leicester]

Enter Kent, Gloucester, and Edmund.

Kent. I thought the king had more affected the
Duke of Albany than Cornwall.

Glo. It did always seem so to us; but now, in the
division of the kingdom, it appears not which of the
dukes he values most, for equalities are so weighed
that curiosity in neither can make choice of either's
moiety.

Kent. Is not this your son, my lord?   8

Glo. His breeding, sir, hath been at my charge. I
have so often blushed to acknowledge him, that now
I am brazed to it.

Kent. I cannot conceive you.   12

Glo. Sir, this young fellow's mother could; whereupon she grew round-wombed and had, indeed, sir,
a son for her cradle ere she had a husband for her
bed. Do you smell a fault?   16

Kent. I cannot wish the fault undone, the issue of
it being so proper.

Glo. But I have a son, sir, by order of law, some

S.d. King Lear's Palace; *cf. n.*   1 affected: *loved*
5, 7 equalities . . . moiety; *cf. n.*
6 curiosity: *whimsicality*   7 moiety: *share*
11 brazed: *hardened*   18 proper: *handsome*

year elder than this, who yet is no dearer in my account. Though this knave came something saucily into the world before he was sent for, yet was his mother fair. There was good sport at his making, and the whoreson must be acknowledged.—Do you know this noble gentleman, Edmund?   25

Edm. No, my lord.

Glo. My Lord of Kent. Remember him hereafter as my honorable friend.

Edm. My services to your lordship.

Kent. I must love you, and sue to know you better.

Edm. Sir, I shall study deserving.   32

Glo. He hath been out nine years, and away he shall again. The king is coming.

Sound a sennet. Enter one bearing a coronet; then Lear, then the Dukes of Albany and Cornwall, next Goneril, Regan, Cordelia with followers.

Lear. Attend the Lords of France and Burgundy, Gloucester.

Glo. I shall, my liege.   *Exit* [*with Edmund*].

Lear. Meantime we shall express our darker purpose.
Give me the map there. Know we have divided
In three our kingdom; and 'tis our fast intent

19 some year: *about a year*   21 something: *rather*
21, 24 knave, whoreson: *terms of bluff affection*
30 sue: *beg*   32 study deserving: *try to be worthy*
33 out: *out of the kingdom*
34 S.d. sennet: *notes on a trumpet*
37 express: *manifest by external tokens*   our darker purpose:
  my purpose which is still somewhat unclarified
37–55 Cf. *n.*   39 fast intent: *fixed purpose*

To shake all cares and business from our age,   40
Conferring them on younger strengths ⟨while we
Unburthen'd crawl toward death. Our son of Cornwall,
And you, our no less loving son of Albany,
We have this hour a constant will to publish   44
Our daughters' several dowers, that future strife
May be prevented now.⟩ The «two great» princes, France
    and Burgundy,
Great rivals in our youngest daughter's love,
Long in our court have made their amorous sojourn,   48
And here are to be answer'd. Tell me, my daughters,
⟨Since now we will divest us both of rule,
Interest of territory, cares of state,⟩
Which of you shall we say doth love us most,   52
That we our largest bounty may extend
Where nature doth with merit challenge. Goneril,
Our eldest-born, speak first.

    Gon.   Sir,
I love you more than word can wield the matter;   56
Dearer than eyesight, space, and liberty;
Beyond what can be valu'd, rich or rare;
No less than life with grace, health, beauty, honor;
As much as child e'er lov'd, or father found;   60
A love that makes breath poor and speech unable;
Beyond all manner of so much I love you.

41–46 while we . . . now; *not in Quarto. See Textual Note.*
45 several: *respective*
46 prevented: *forestalled*   two great; *not in Folio. See Textual*
    Note.   France and Burgundy; *cf. n.*
51 Interest: *legal title*
54 Where . . . challenge; *cf. n.*
57 space: *the external world*   59 with: *enhanced by*
60 found: *experienced*   61 unable: *impotent*

Cor. [*aside*]. What shall Cordelia speak? Love, and be
    silent.

    Lear. Of all these bounds, even from this line to
    this,   64
With shadowy forests and ⟨with champains rich'd,
With plenteous rivers and⟩ wide-skirted meads,
We make thee lady. To thine and Albany's issues
Be this perpetual. What says our second daughter,   68
Our dearest Regan, wife of Cornwall? «Speak.»

    Reg. I am made of that self metal as my sister,
And prize me at her worth. In my true heart
I find she names my very deed of love.   72
Only she comes too short, that I profess
Myself an enemy to all other joys
Which the most precious square of sense possesses
And find I am alone felicitate   76
In your dear highness' love.

    Cor. [*aside*].   Then, poor Cordelia!
And yet not so, since I am sure my love's
More richer than my tongue.

    Lear. To thee and thine, hereditary ever,   80
Remain this ample third of our fair kingdom,
No less in space, validity, and pleasure,
Than that conferr'd on Goneril. Now, our joy,
Although our last and least, to whose young love   84
⟨The vines of France and milk of Burgundy

---

70 self: *same*
71 prize . . . worth: *esteem myself as worthy as she is*
72 Cf. *n.*
73 Only: *only in this*
75 square; cf. *n.*   76 felicitate: *made happy*
79 More richer; cf. *n.*   82 validity: *value*
84 Cf. *n.*   85 milk: *pasture land*

Strive to be interess'd) what can you say to draw
A third more opulent than your sisters? ⟨Speak.⟩

    Cor. Nothing, my lord.   88

    ⟨*Lear.* Nothing?

    Cor. Nothing.⟩

    Lear. Nothing will come of nothing. Speak again.

    Cor. Unhappy that I am, I cannot heave   92
My heart into my mouth. I love your majesty
According to my bond; no more nor less.

    Lear. How, how, Cordelia! Mend your speech a little,
Lest you may mar your fortunes.   96

    Cor.   Good my lord,
You have begot me, bred me, lov'd me. I
Return those duties back as are right fit,
Obey you, love you, and most honor you.
Why have my sisters husbands, if they say   100
They love you all? Haply, when I shall wed,
That lord whose hand must take my plight shall carry
Half my love with him, half my care and duty.
Sure I shall never marry like my sisters   104
«To love my father all».

    Lear. But goes thy heart with this?

    Cor.   Ay, my good lord.

    Lear. So young, and so untender?

    Cor. So young, my lord, and true.   108

    Lear. Let it be so. Thy truth then be thy dower,
For by the sacred radiance of the sun,
The mysteries of Hecate and the night,

---

86 interess'd: *given a share*
94 bond: *obligation of duty*
101 all: *exclusively*   102 plight: *pledge*
111 Hecate: *goddess of witchcraft*

By all the operation of the orbs   112
From whom we do exist and cease to be,
Here I disclaim all my paternal care,
Propinquity and property of blood,
And as a stranger to my heart and me   116
Hold thee from this for ever. The barbarous Scythian,
Or he that makes his generation messes
To gorge his appetite, shall ⟨to my bosom⟩
Be as well neighbor'd, pitied, and reliev'd,   120
As thou, my sometime daughter.

    Kent.   Good my liege!—
    Lear. Peace, Kent!
Come not between the dragon and his wrath.
I lov'd her most, and thought to set my rest   124
On her kind nursery. Hence, and avoid my sight!
So be my grave my peace, as here I give
Her father's heart from her! Call France. Who stirs?
Call Burgundy.—Cornwall and Albany,   128
With my two daughters' dowers digest the third.
Let pride, which she calls plainness, marry her.
I do invest you jointly with my power,
Pre-eminence, and all the large effects   132
That troop with majesty. Ourself by monthly course,
With reservation of an hundred knights,

112 operation: *planetary influence*
115 property of blood: *kinship*
117 this: *this time*   118 generation: *children*
119 to my bosom: *in my affections*
120 neighbor'd: *held in friendly regard*
124 set my rest: *stake my all (figure from a game)*
125 nursery: *nursing*   129 digest: *assimilate*
130 plainness: *frankness*   marry: *find a husband for*
132 effects: *outward marks of royalty*
133 troop with: *follow in the train of*   course: *rotation*

By you to be sustain'd, shall our abode
Make with you by due turn. Only we still retain   136
The name and all th' additions to a king.
The sway,
Revénue, execution of the rest,
Beloved sons, be yours: which to confirm,   140
This coronet part between you.

   Kent.   Royal Lear,
Whom I have ever honor'd as my king,
Lov'd as my father, as my master follow'd,
As my great patron thought on in my prayers,—

   Lear. The bow is bent and drawn. Make from the
       shaft.   145

   Kent. Let it fall rather, though the fork invade
The region of my heart. Be Kent unmannerly
When Lear is mad. What wouldst thou do, old man?   148
Think'st thou that duty shall have dread to speak
When power to flattery bows? To plainness honor's bound
When majesty stoops to folly. Reverse thy doom,
And in thy best consideration check   152
This hideous rashness. Answer my life my judgment:
Thy youngest daughter does not love thee least;
Nor are those empty-hearted whose low sounds
Reverb no hollowness.

   Lear.   Kent, on thy life, no more.   156

   Kent. My life I never held but as a pawn

---

136 still; *cf. n.*
137 additions: *titles, marks of distinction*
138 The sway; *cf. n.*   141 coronet; *cf. n.*
145 Make from: *get out of the way of*   151 *Cf. n.*
152 in . . . consideration: *with all the care you can*
153 Answer my life: *let my life answer for*
156 Reverb: *re-echo; cf. n.*

To wage against thine enemies; nor fear to lose it,
Thy safety being the motive.

    Lear.   Out of my sight!

    Kent. See better, Lear, and let me still remain   160
The true blank of thine eye.

    Lear. Now, by Apollo,—

    Kent.   Now, by Apollo, king,
Thou swear'st thy gods in vain.

    Lear.   O vassal! miscreant!

                 [*Laying his hand on his sword.*]

⟨*Alb.*⟩
⟨*Corn.*⟩ } Dear sir, forbear.⟩   164

    Kent. «Do;»
Kill thy physician, and thy fee bestow
Upon the foul disease. Revoke thy doom,
Or whilst I can vent clamor from my throat,   168
I'll tell thee thou dost evil.

    Lear.   Hear me, ⟨recreant!⟩
On thine allegiance, hear me!
That thou hast sought to make us break our vow,
Which we durst never yet, and with strain'd pride   172
To come betwixt our sentence and our power
(Which nor our nature nor our place can bear):
Our potency made good, take thy reward.
Five days we do allot thee for provision   176
To shield thee from diseases of the world,
And on the sixth to turn thy hated back

---

158 wage: *stake*   160 still: *always*
161 blank: *white spot in center of target*
162 by Apollo; *cf. n.*   163 vassal! miscreant; *cf. n.*
171 That; *cf. n.*   us; *cf. n.*
175 Our . . . good; *cf. n.*   176 Five days; *cf. n.*
177 diseases: *slight vexations, dis-eases; cf. n.*

Upon our kingdom. If on the tenth day following
Thy banish'd trunk be found in our dominions,   180
The moment is thy death. Away! By Jupiter,
This shall not be revok'd.

    Kent. Fare thee well, king. Sith thus thou wilt appear,
Freedom lives hence, and banishment is here.   184
[*To Cordelia.*] The gods to their dear shelter take thee,
    maid,
That justly think'st, and hast most rightly said!
[*To Regan and Goneril.*] And your large speeches may
    your deeds approve,
That good effects may spring from words of love.   188
Thus Kent, O princes, bids you all adieu;
He'll shape his old course in a country new.   *Exit.*

Flourish. Enter Gloucester with France and
Burgundy, Attendants.

    Glo. Here's France and Burgundy, my noble lord.
    Lear. My Lord of Burgundy,   192
We first address toward you, who with this king
Hath rivall'd for our daughter. What, in the least,
Will you require in present dower with her,
Or cease your quest of love?
    Bur.   Most royal majesty,   196
I crave no more than hath your highness offer'd,
Nor will you tender less.

---

180 trunk: *body*   182 revok'd; *cf. n.*
183 Sith: *since*   thus: *i.e., in the character of a despot*
187 approve: *make good; cf. n.*
188 effects: *(actual) results*   words: *(mere) words*
190 shape . . . course: *be his old self*
S.d. Flourish: *music of horns*
194 in the least: *at the lowest estimate*   198 tender: *offer*

Lear.   Right noble Burgundy,
When she was dear t'us we did hold her so,
But now her price is fall'n. Sir, there she stands.   200
If aught within that little-seeming substance,
Or all of it, with our displeasure piec'd,
And nothing more, may fitly like your Grace,
She's there, and she is yours.

Bur.   I know no answer.   204

Lear. Will you, with those infirmities she owes,
Unfriended, new-adopted to our hate,
Dower'd with our curse, and stranger'd with our oath,
Take her or leave her?

Bur.   Pardon me, royal sir;   208
Election makes not up in such conditions.

Lear. Then leave her, sir; for, by the power that made
    me,
I tell you all her wealth.—[*To France.*] For you, great
    king,
I would not from your love make such a stray   212
To match you where I hate. Therefore, beseech you
T'avert your liking a more worthier way
Than on a wretch whom nature is asham'd
Almost t'acknowledge hers.

France.   This is most strange!   216
That she, that even but now was your best object,
The argument of your praise, balm of your age,
Most best, most dearest, should in this trice of time

201 *Cf. n.*   202 piec'd: *pieced out, amplified*
203 fitly like: *properly satisfy*   205 owes: *owns*
207 stranger'd with: *made a stranger by (cf. line 116)*
209 Election, etc.: *I cannot choose*
212 stray: *wandering, truancy*
218 argument: *subject*   219 trice: *moment*

Commit a thing so monstrous to dismantle   220
So many folds of favor. Sure, her offence
Must be of such unnatural degree
That monsters it, or your fore-vouch'd affection
Fall'n into taint;—which to believe of her   224
Must be a faith that reason without miracle
Could never plant in me.

    Cor.   I yet beseech your majesty—
If for I want that glib and oily art
To speak and purpose not (since what I well intend,   228
I'll do't before I speak)—that you make known
It is no vicious blot, murther, or foulness,
No únchaste action or dishonor'd step,
That hath depriv'd me of your grace and favor,   232
But even for want of that for which I am richer,
A still-soliciting eye, and such a tongue
That I am glad I have not, though not to have it
Hath lost me in your liking.

    Lear.   Better thou   236
Hadst not been born than not t'have pleas'd me better.

    France. Is it but this? a tardiness in nature
Which often leaves the history unspoke
That it intends to do? My Lord of Burgundy,   240
What say you to the lady? Love's not love
When it is mingled with regards that stands

---

220 to dismantle: *as to strip off*
221 folds of favor: *layers of regard; cf. n.*
223 monsters it: *makes it abnormal*
224 Fall'n into taint: *become blemished*   which; *cf. n.*
228 speak and purpose not: *speak deceitfully*   what . . .
    intend: *i.e., when I have a good intention*
230 murther; *cf. n.*   234 still-soliciting: *perpetually greedy*
241 to: *on the subject of*   242 stands: *(old plural form)*

Aloof from th'entire point. Will you have her?
She is herself a dowry.

  Bur.   Royal King,   244
Give but that portion which yourself propos'd,
And here I take Cordelia by the hand,
Duchess of Burgundy.

  Lear. Nothing. I have sworn ⟨I am firm⟩. 248

  Bur. [*to Cor.*]. I am sorry, then, you have so lost a
   father
That you must lose a husband.

  Cor.   Peace be with Burgundy!
Since that respects of fortune are his love,
I shall not be his wife.   252

  France. Fairest Cordelia, that art most rich, being poor;
Most choice, forsaken; and most lov'd, despis'd!
Thee and thy virtues here I seize upon.
Be it lawful, I take up what's cast away. 256
Gods, gods! 'Tis strange that from their cold'st neglect
My love should kindle to inflam'd respect.
Thy dowerless daughter, king, thrown to my chance,
Is queen of us, of ours, and our fair France: 260
Not all the dukes of waterish Burgundy
Can buy this unpriz'd precious maid of me.
Bid them farewell, Cordelia, though unkind.
Thou losest here, a better where to find. 264

  Lear. Thou hast her, France. Let her be thine, for we
Have no such daughter, nor shall ever see
That face of hers again. Therefore be gone

251 respects: *considerations*
258 inflam'd respect: *warmest deference*
262 unpriz'd precious: *precious though unprized*
264 a better where: *a better place*

Without our grace, our love, our benison.   268
Come, noble Burgundy.

> *Flourish. Exeunt Lear and Burgundy [Cornwall,*
> *Albany, Gloucester, and Attendants].*

France. Bid farewell to your sisters.

Cor. The jewels of our father, with wash'd eyes
Cordelia leaves you. I know you what you are;   272
And like a sister am most loath to call
Your faults as they are nam'd. Use well our father.
To your professed bosoms I commit him;
But yet, alas, stood I within his grace,   276
I would prefer him to a better place.
So farewell to you both.

Gon. Prescribe not us our duties.

Reg.   Let your study
Be to content your lord, who hath receiv'd you
At fortune's alms. You have obedience scanted,
And well are worth the want that you have wanted. 282

Cor. Time shall unfold what plighted cunning hides;
Who covers faults, at last shame them derides.
Well may you prosper!

France.   Come, my fair Cordelia.

>   *Ex. France and Cordelia.*

Gon. Sister, it is not little I have to say of what

---

268 benison: *blessing*
271 The jewels; *cf. n.*   wash'd eyes: *eyes that see clearly*
273 like a sister: *as befits a sister*
274 as . . . nam'd: *by their right names*
275 your professed bosoms: *the affections you have professed*
277 prefer: *commend*
281 At fortune's alms: *as a petty gift of chance*
282 well . . . wanted; *cf. n.*   283 plighted: *folded; cf. n.*

most nearly appertains to us both. I think our father
will hence to-night.   288

Reg. That's most certain, and with you. Next
month with us.

Gon. You see how full of changes his age is. The
observation we have made of it hath not been little.
He always loved our sister most; and with what
poor judgment he hath now cast her off appears too
grossly.

Reg. 'Tis the infirmity of his age. Yet he hath
ever but slenderly known himself.   297

Gon. The best and soundest of his time hath been
but rash. Then must we look from his age to receive not alone the imperfections of long-engraffed
condition, but therewithal the unruly waywardness
that infirm and choleric years bring with them.   302

Reg. Such unconstant starts are we like to have
from him as this of Kent's banishment.

Gon. There is further compliment of leavetaking
between France and him; pray you, let us sit together.
If our father carry authority with such disposition as
he bears, this last surrender of his will but offend
us.   309

Reg. We shall further think of it.

Gon. We must do something, and i' th' heat.

                                                Exeunt.

---

295 grossly: *obviously*   298 time: *years*
300 engraffed condition: *implanted temperament*
303 starts: *fits of temper*   305 compliment of: *ceremonious*
306 sit; *cf. n.*   308 offend: *harm*

SCENE SECOND

[Earl of Gloucester's Castle]

Enter Bastard, solus.

Edm. Thou, Nature, art my goddess. To thy law
My services are bound. Wherefore should I
Stand in the plague of custom, and permit
The curiosity of nations to deprive me,   4
For that I am some twelve or fourteen moonshines
Lag of a brother? Why bastard? wherefore base?
When my dimensions are as well compact,
My mind as generous, and my shape as true   8
As honest madam's issue? Why brand they us
With base? with baseness? bastardy? base, base?
Who in the lusty stealth of nature take
More composition and fierce quality   12
Than doth, within a dull, stale, tired bed,
Go to th'creating a whole tribe of fops,
Got 'tween asleep and wake? Well then,
Legitimate Edgar, I must have your land.   16
Our father's love is to the bastard Edmund
As to th'legitimate. Fine word, 'legitimate'!
Well, my legitimate, if this letter speed
And my invention thrive, Edmund the base   20
Shall taw th'legitimate. I grow, I prosper;
Now, gods, stand up for bastards!

3 Stand . . . plague: *submit to the nuisance*
4 curiosity: *pedantry, legal hair-splitting*
6 Lag of: *behind*   12 composition: *symmetry*
14 fops: *fools*   19 speed: *succeed*

Enter Gloucester.

[*Edmund ostentatiously reading a letter.*]

Glo. Kent banished thus, and France in choler parted!
And the king gone to-night, prescrib'd his power,   24
Confin'd to exhibition! All this done
Upon the gad! Edmund, how now? What news?

Edm. So please your lordship, none.

Glo. Why so earnestly seek you to put up that
letter?   29

Edm. I know no news, my lord.

Glo. What paper were you reading?

Edm. Nothing, my lord.   32

Glo. No? What needed then that terrible dispatch
of it into your pocket? The quality of nothing hath
not such need to hide itself. Let's see. Come! If it be
nothing, I shall not need spectacles.   36

Edm. I beseech you, sir, pardon me. It is a letter
from my brother that I have not all o'erread, and for
so much as I have perused, I find it not fit for your
o'erlooking.   40

Glo. Give me the letter, sir.

Edm. I shall offend, either to detain or give it.
The contents, as in part I understand them, are too
blame.   44

Glo. Let's see! let's see!

Edm. I hope, for my brother's justification, he
wrote this but as an essay or taste of my virtue.   47

---

21 taw: *whip, flog, thrash; cf. n.*
24 prescrib'd: *limited; cf. n.*
25 exhibition: *allowance, maintenance*
26 gad: *spur*   What news; *cf. n.*
43 too blame; *cf. n.*   47 essay: *trial*

Glo. reads.

This policy and reverence of age makes the world bitter
to the best of our times, keeps our fortunes from us till our
oldness cannot relish them. I begin to find an idle and fond
bondage in the oppression of aged tyranny, who sways, not
as it hath power, but as it is suffered. Come to me, that of
this I may speak more. If our father would sleep till I waked
him, you should enjoy half his revenue for ever, and live
the beloved of your brother,

Edgar.

—Hum! Conspiracy! 'Sleep till I waked him, you
should enjoy half his revenue.'—My son Edgar! Had
he a hand to write this? a heart and brain to breed it
in? When came this to you? Who brought it?　　60

Edm. It was not brought me, my lord; there's the
cunning of it. I found it thrown in at the casement
of my closet.

Glo. You know the character to be your brother's?

Edm. If the matter were good, my lord, I durst
swear it were his; but, in respect of that, I would fain
think it were not.　　67

Glo. It is his.

Edm. It is his hand, my lord; but I hope his heart
is not in the contents.

Glo. Has he never before sounded you in this business?　　72

Edm. Never, my lord: but I have heard him oft
maintain it to be fit that, sons at perfect age and

48 policy and reverence of: *policy of revering*
50 fond: *foolish*　　　　62, 63 thrown . . . closet; *cf. n.*
63 closet: *private room*　　　64 character: *handwriting*
66 in respect of that: *considering the nature of the 'matter' or contents*
66 fain: *gladly*　　　　　　74 sons: *sons being*

fathers declined, the father should be as ward to the
son, and the son manage his revenue.   76

Glo. O villain, villain! His very opinion in the
letter! Abhorred villain! Unnatural, detested, brutish
villain! worse than brutish! Go, sirrah, seek him; I'll
apprehend him. Abominable villain! Where is he?   80

Edm. I do not well know, my lord. If it shall
please you to suspend your indignation against my
brother till you can derive from him better testimony of his intent, you should run a certain course;
where, if you violently proceed against him, mis-
taking his purpose, it would make a great gap in your
own honor, and shake in pieces the heart of his obedience. I dare pawn down my life for him, that he hath
writ this to feel my affection to your Honor, and to
no other pretence of danger.   90

Glo. Think you so?

Edm. If your Honor judge it meet, I will place you
where you shall hear us confer of this, and by an
auricular assurance have your satisfaction; and that
without any further delay than this very evening.   95

Glo. He cannot be such a monster—

«*Edm.* Nor is not, sure.

Glo.—to his father, that so tenderly and entirely
loves him. Heaven and earth!» Edmund, seek him
out; wind me into him, I pray you. Frame the business after your own wisdom. I would unstate myself
to be in a due resolution.

---

78 detested: *detestable*   80 apprehend: *arrest*
84 should; *cf. n.*   90 pretence: *intention*
92, 93 I will . . . this; *cf. n.*   100 wind me into him; *cf. n.*
101 unstate myself: *give all I am and have*
102 due resolution: *proper certainty*

Edm. I will seek him, sir, presently, convey the business as I shall find means, and acquaint you withal.   105

Glo. These late eclipses in the sun and moon portend no good to us. Though the wisdom of nature can reason it thus and thus, yet nature finds itself scourged by the sequent effects. Love cools, friendship falls off, brothers divide. In cities, mutinies; in countries, discord; in palaces, treason; and the bond cracked 'twixt son and father. ⟨This villain of mine comes under the prediction; there's son against father. The king falls from bias of nature; there's father against child. We have seen the best of our time: machinations, hollowness, treachery, and all ruinous disorders, follow us disquietly to our graves.⟩ Find out this villain, Edmund. It shall lose thee nothing. Do it carefully. And the noble and true-hearted Kent banished! his offence, honesty! 'Tis strange!   *Exit.*

Edm. This is the excellent foppery of the world, that, when we are sick in fortune—often the surfeits of our own behavior—we make guilty of our disasters the sun, the moon, and the stars; as if we were villains on necessity, fools by heavenly compulsion, knaves, thieves, and treachers by spherical predomi-

---

103 presently: *instantly*   convey: *manage (with privacy and discretion)*
105 withal: *therewith*
106 These late eclipses; *cf. n.*
107 wisdom of nature: *natural philosophy*
108 nature: *human nature, the world of man*
109 sequent effects: *results that follow the eclipses; cf. n.*
114 falls . . . nature; *cf. n.*
121 excellent foppery: *exceeding folly*
126 treachers: *traitors*   spherical predominance: *causative action of the celestial 'spheres'*

nance, drunkards, liars, and adulterers by an enforced
obedience of planetary influence, and all that we are
evil in by a divine thrusting on: an admirable eva-
sion of whoremaster man, to lay his goatish disposition on the charge of a star! My father compounded
with my mother under the dragon's tail, and my
nativity was under *ursa major;* so that it follows I am
rough and lecherous. «Fut!» I should have been that
I am had the maidenliest star in the firmament
twinkled on my bastardizing. «Edgar—»   136

Enter Edgar.

Pat he comes, like the catastrophe of the old comedy.
My cue is villainous melancholy, with a sigh like
Tom o' Bedlam.—O, these eclipses do portend these
divisions! ⟨*Fa, sol, la, mi.*⟩

Edg. How now, brother Edmund! What serious
contemplation are you in?   142

Edm. I am thinking, brother, of a prediction I read
this other day, what should follow these eclipses.

Edg. Do you busy yourself with that?   145

Edm. I promise you the effects he writes of succeed unhappily; ⟨as of unnaturalness between the
child and the parent, death, dearth, dissolutions of
ancient amities, divisions in state, menaces and male-
dictions against king and nobles, needless diffidences,
banishment of friends, dissipation of cohorts, nuptial
breaches, and I know not what.   152

129 thrusting on: *impulsion*
131 charge: *liability*   132 dragon's tail; *cf. n.*
133 *ursa major: the Great Bear*   140 *Fa, sol, la, mi; cf. n.*
150 diffidences: *suspicions*
151 dissipation of cohorts: *disaffection in the army*

Edg. How long have you been a sectary astronomical?

Edm. Come, come! ⟩ When saw you my father last?   156

Edg. The night gone by.

Edm. Spake you with him?

Edg. Ay, two hours together.

Edm. Parted you in good terms? Found you no displeasure in him by word nor countenance?

Edg. None at all.   162

Edm. Bethink yourself wherein you may have offended him; and at my entreaty forbear his presence until some little time hath qualified the heat of his displeasure, which at this instant so rageth in him that with the mischief of your person it would scarcely allay.   168

Edg. Some villain hath done me wrong.

Edm. That's my fear. ⟨I pray you have a continent forbearance till the speed of his rage goes slower, and, as I say, retire with me to my lodging, from whence I will fitly bring you to hear my lord speak. Pray ye, go; there's my key. If you do stir abroad, go armed.   175

Edg. Armed, brother?

Edm.⟩ Brother, I advise you to the best; «go armed;» I am no honest man if there be any good meaning toward you. I have told you what I have seen and heard, but faintly. Nothing like the image and horror of it. Pray you, away.

---

153 sectary astronomical: *member of the astronomical sect*
167 mischief: *harm*   170 continent: *temperate*
180 image and horror: *horrible image*

Edg. Shall I hear from you anon?

Edm. I do serve you in this business.   183

Exit Edgar.

A credulous father and a brother noble,
Whose nature is so far from doing harms
That he suspects none, on whose foolish honesty
My practices ride easy! I see the business.   187
Let me, if not by birth, have lands by wit.
All with me's meet that I can fashion fit.   *Exit.*

SCENE THIRD

[Duke of Albany's Palace, York(?)]

Enter Goneril, and [Oswald her] Steward.

Gon. Did my father strike my gentleman for chiding of his fool?

Osw. Ay, madam.

Gon. By day and night he wrongs me. Every hour   4
He flashes into one gross crime or other
That sets us all at odds. I'll not endure it.
His knights grow riotous, and himself upbraids us
On every trifle. When he returns from hunting,
I will not speak with him. Say I am sick.   9
If you come slack of former services,
You shall do well. The fault of it I'll answer.

Osw. He's coming, madam. I hear him.   12

Gon. Put on what weary negligence you please,

187 practices: *treacherous plots*   189 *Cf. n.*
Scene Third. S.d. *Duke of Albany's Palace; cf. n.*
5 crime: *offence*

You and your fellows. I'd have it come to question.
If he distaste it, let him to my sister,
Whose mind and mine, I know, in that are one,   16
«Not to be over-rul'd. Idle old man,
That still would manage those authorities
That he hath given away! Now, by my life,
Old fools are babes again, and must be us'd   20
With checks as flatteries, when they are seen abus'd.»
Remember what I have said.

    Osw.   Well, madam.

    Gon. And let his knights have colder looks among you.
What grows of it, no matter. Advise your fellows so.   24
«I would breed from hence occasions, and I shall,
That I may speak.» I'll write straight to my sister
To hold my very course. Prepare for dinner.

                               Exeunt.

SCENE FOURTH

[*The same*]

Enter Kent [disguised].

    Kent. If but as well I other accents borrow,
That can my speech defuse, my good intent
May carry through itself to that full issue
For which I raz'd my likeness. Now, banish'd Kent,   4

14 question: *discussion*   17 Idle: *foolish*
21 With . . . abus'd; *cf. n.*   22 Well: *like French 'bien'*
1 *Cf. n.*   2 defuse: *disguise, disorder*
3 carry through: *accomplish*   issue: *conclusion*
4 raz'd: *erased*

If thou canst serve where thou dost stand condemn'd,
So may it come, thy master whom thou lov'st
Shall find thee full of labors.

Horns within. Enter Lear and Attendants.

Lear. Let me not stay a jot for dinner. Go, get it
ready. [*Exit an Attendant.*] How now! what art
thou?   10

Kent. A man, sir.

Lear. What dost thou profess? What wouldst thou
with us?

Kent. I do profess to be no less than I seem; to serve
him truly that will put me in trust, to love him that
is honest, to converse with him that is wise and says
little, to fear judgment, to fight when I cannot
choose, and to eat no fish.

Lear. What art thou?   19

Kent. A very honest-hearted fellow, and as poor as
the king.

Lear. If thou be'st as poor for a subject as he's for
a king, thou art poor enough. What wouldst thou?

Kent. Service.   24

Lear. Whom wouldst thou serve?

Kent. You.

Lear. Dost thou know me, fellow?   27

Kent. No, sir; but you have that in your countenance which I would fain call master.

Lear. What's that?

Kent. Authority.

Lear. What services canst thou do?   32

12 dost . . . profess: *is thy profession*
18 fish; *cf. n.*   19 *Cf. n.*

Kent. I can keep honest counsel, ride, run, mar a curious tale in telling it, and deliver a plain message bluntly. That which ordinary men are fit for, I am qualified in, and the best of me is diligence.   36

Lear. How old art thou?

Kent. Not so young, sir, to love a woman for singing, nor so old to dote on her for anything. I have years on my back forty-eight.   40

Lear. Follow me; thou shalt serve me, if I like thee no worse after dinner. I will not part from thee yet. Dinner, ho! dinner! Where's my knave, my fool? Go you and call my fool hither.   [*Exit an Attendant.*]

Enter Steward [Oswald].

You, you, sirrah, where's my daughter?   45

Osw. So please you,—   *Exit.*

Lear. What says the fellow there? Call the clot-poll back. [*Exit a Knight.*] Where's my fool? Ho! I think the world's asleep. [*Re-enter Knight.*] How now? where's that mongrel?   50

Knight. He says, my lord, your daughter is not well.

Lear. Why came not the slave back to me when I called him?   54

Knight. Sir, he answered me in the roundest manner, he would not.

Lear. He would not!   57

Knight. My lord, I know not what the matter is; but, to my judgment, your highness is not entertained with that ceremonious affection as you were

---

34 curious: *fanciful*
40 forty-eight; *cf. n.*   47 clotpoll: *blockhead, clodpole*

wont. There's a great abatement of kindness appears as well in the general dependants as in the duke himself also and your daughter.

Lear. Ha! sayest thou so?   64

Knight. I beseech you, pardon me, my lord, if I be mistaken; for my duty cannot be silent when I think your highness wronged.   67

Lear. Thou but remember'st me of mine own conception. I have perceived a most faint neglect of late, which I have rather blamed as mine own jealous curiosity than as a very pretence and purpose of unkindness. I will look further into't. But where's my fool? I have not seen him this two days.   73

Knight. Since my young lady's going into France, sir, the fool hath much pined away.

Lear. No more of that. I have noted it well. Go you and tell my daughter I would speak with her.

                                        [*Exit Knight.*]

Go you, call hither my fool.   [*Exit an Attendant.*]

                Enter Steward [*Oswald*].

O! you sir, you, come you hither, sir. Who am I, sir?

Osw. My lady's father.   80

Lear. 'My lady's father!' my lord's knave! You whoreson dog! you slave! you cur!

Osw. I am none of these, my lord; I beseech your pardon.

61 kindness: *courtesy*
68 remember'st . . . conception; *cf. n.*
69 faint: *sluggish*
70 jealous curiosity: *suspicious punctiliousness*
71 very pretence: *genuine intention*

Lear. Do you bandy looks with me, you rascal?

[*Striking him.*]

Osw. I'll not be strucken, my lord.   86

Kent. Nor tripped neither, you base football player.   [*Tripping up his heels.*]

Lear. I thank thee, fellow. Thou serv'st me, and I'll love thee.   90

Kent. Come, sir, arise, away! I'll teach you differences! Away, away! If you will measure your lubber's length again, tarry. But away! Go to! have you wisdom? [*Pushes Oswald out.*] So.

Lear. Now, my friendly knave, I thank thee. There's earnest of thy service.   96

[*Gives him money.*]

Enter Fool.

Fool. Let me hire him too. Here's my coxcomb.

Lear. How now, my pretty knave! how dost thou?

Fool. Sirrah, you were best take my coxcomb.

«*Kent.* Why, fool?»   100

⟨*Lear.* Why, my boy?⟩

Fool. Why, for taking one's part that's out of favor. Nay, an thou canst not smile as the wind sits, thou'lt catch cold shortly. There, take my coxcomb. Why, this fellow has banished two on's daughters, and did the third a blessing against his will. If thou follow him, thou must needs wear my coxcomb. How now,

85 bandy: *exchange (an expression from the game of tennis)*
86 strucken: *(mainly a Northern form)*
87 football; *cf. n.*   91 differences: *quibbling distinctions*
96 earnest: *advance wages*
97 coxcomb: *fool's cap*
103 an: *if*

100, 101 *Cf. n.*
105 on's: *of his*

nuncle! Would I had two coxcombs and two daughters!

Lear. Why, my boy?   110

Fool. If I gave them all my living, I'd keep my coxcombs myself. There's mine [*offering the coxcomb to Lear*]; beg another of thy daughters.

Lear. Take heed, sirrah! the whip.   114

Fool. Truth's a dog must to kennel. He must be whipped out when the Lady-brach may stand by the fire and stink.

Lear. A pestilent gall to me!

Fool. Sirrah, I'll teach thee a speech.   119

Lear. Do.

Fool. Mark it, nuncle:—

> Have more than thou showest,   122
> Speak less than thou knowest,
> Lend less than thou owest,
> Ride more than thou goest,
> Learn more than thou trowest,   126
> Set less than thou throwest.
> Leave thy drink and thy whore,
> And keep in-a-door,
> And thou shalt have more   130
> Than two tens to a score.

Kent. This is nothing, fool.

Fool. Then 'tis like the breath of an unfee'd lawyer. You gave me nothing for 't.—Can you make no use of nothing, nuncle?   135

108 nuncle: *mine uncle*   116 brach: *hunting-bitch; cf. n.*
118 *Cf. n.*   122–126 have . . . trowest; *cf. n.*
125 goest: *walkest*   126 trowest: *believest*
127 Set . . . throwest: *stake less than you throw to win*
129 keep in-a-door: *stay at home and tend to your business*
130, 131 *Cf. n.*

Lear. Why, no, boy; nothing can be made out of nothing.

Fool [to Kent]. Prithee, tell him, so much the rent of his land comes to. He will not believe a fool.

Lear. A bitter fool!   140

Fool. Dost thou know the difference, my boy, between a bitter fool and a sweet one?

Lear. No, lad. Teach me.

Fool.

«That lord that counsell'd thee
    To give away thy land,   145
Come place him here by me.
    Do thou for him stand.
The sweet and bitter fool
    Will presently appear;   149
The one in motley here,
    The other found out there.

Lear. Dost thou call me fool, boy?

Fool. All thy other titles thou hast given away. That thou wast born with.   154

Kent. This is not altogether fool, my lord.

Fool. No, faith! Lords and great men will not let me. If I had a monopoly out, they would have part on't, and ladies too. They will not let me have all the fool to myself; they'll be snatching.» Nuncle, give me an egg, and I'll give thee two crowns.   160

Lear. What two crowns shall they be?

Fool. Why, after I have cut the egg i' th' middle and eat up the meat, the two crowns of the egg. When thou clovest thy crown i' th' middle and gav'st away both parts, thou bor'st thine ass on thy back

136, 137 nothing . . . nothing; *cf.* I.i.91   147 *Cf. n.*
157 monopoly out; *cf. n.*   163 crowns: *half-shells*

o'er the dirt. Thou hadst little wit in thy bald crown when thou gav'st thy golden one away. If I speak like myself in this, let him be whipped that first finds it so.   169

> Fools had ne'er less grace in a year,
>   For wise men are grown foppish,
> And know not how their wits to wear,   172
>   Their manners are so apish.

Lear. When were you wont to be so full of songs, sirrah?   175

Fool. I have used it, nuncle, e'er since thou mad'st thy daughters thy mothers; for when thou gav'st them the rod and putt'st down thine own breeches,

> Then they for sudden joy did weep,   179
>   And I for sorrow sung,
> That such a king should play bo-peep,
>   And go the fools among.

Prithee, nuncle, keep a schoolmaster that can teach thy fool to lie. I would fain learn to lie.   184

Lear. An you lie, sirrah, we'll have you whipped.

Fool. I marvel what kin thou and thy daughters are. They'll have me whipped for speaking true, thou'lt have me whipped for lying; and sometimes I am whipped for holding my peace. I had rather be any kind o' thing than a fool; and yet I would not be thee, nuncle. Thou hast pared thy wit o' both sides, and left nothing i' th' middle. Here comes one o' the parings.

168 like myself: *like a fool*
168, 169 let . . . so; *cf. n.*
170 had . . . grace: *were never less in demand*
171 foppish: *fool-like*
172 wits to wear: *display their wisdom; cf. n.*
181 play bo-peep; *cf. n.*

Enter Goneril.

Lear. How now, daughter? what makes that frontlet on? You are too much of late i' th' frown.   194

Fool. Thou wast a pretty fellow when thou hadst
no need to care for her frowning. Now thou art an O
without a figure. I am better than thou art now. I am
a fool, thou art nothing. [*To Goneril.*] Yes, forsooth,
I will hold my tongue. So your face bids me, though
you say nothing.   200

> Mum, mum;
> He that keeps nor crust nor crumb,
> Weary of all, shall want some.

That's a sheeled peascod.   [*Pointing to Lear.*]
Gon. Not only, sir, this your all-licens'd fool,
But other of your insolent retinue   206
Do hourly carp and quarrel, breaking forth
In rank and not-to-be-endured riots.
Sir,
I had thought by making this well known unto you
To have found a safe redress; but now grow fearful,
By what yourself too late have spoke and done,   212
That you protect this course, and put it on
By your allowance; which if you should, the fault
Would not 'scape censure, nor the redresses sleep,
Which, in the tender of a wholesome weal,   216

193 frontlet: *forehead-band; i.e., frown*
196, 197 an O without a figure: *a mere cipher*   203 *Cf. n.*
204 sheeled peascod: *empty peapod*
211 safe redress: *assured remedy*
213 protect: *authorize*   put . . . on: *encourage*
214 allowance: *approval*
216 tender: *care*   wholesome weal: *sound public welfare*

Might in their working do you that offence,
Which else were shame, that then necessity
Will call discreet proceeding.

    Fool. For you know, nuncle,   220

> The hedge-sparrow fed the cuckoo so long,
> That it's had it head bit off by it young.

So out went the candle, and we were left darkling.

    Lear. Are you our daughter?   224

    Gon. I would you would make use of your good wisdom
(Whereof I know you are fraught), and put away
These dispositions which of late transport you
From what you rightly are.   228

    Fool. May not an ass know when the cart draws
the horse? Whoop, Jug! I love thee.

    Lear. Does any here know me? This is not Lear.   231
Does Lear walk thus? speak thus? Where are his eyes?
Either his notion weakens, or his discernings
Are lethargied. Ha! waking? 'tis not so.
Who is it that can tell me who I am?

    Fool. Lear's shadow.   236

    «*Lear.* I would learn that, for by the marks of sov-
ereignty, knowledge and reason, I should be false
persuaded I had daughters.   239

    Fool. Which they will make an obedient father.»
Lear. Your name, fair gentlewoman?

    Gon. This admiration, sir, is much o' th' favor   242
Of other your new pranks. I do beseech you

---

222 it: *its; cf. n.*   223 darkling: *in the dark*
226 fraught: *stored*   230 Whoop . . . thee; *cf. n.*
233 notion: *understanding*   discernings: *faculties by which*
                                  he apprehends (?)
240 Which they; *cf. n.*   242 admiration: *sign of wonder*

To understand my purposes aright,
As you are old and reverend, should be wise.
Here do you keep a hundred knights and squires;   246
Men so disorder'd, so debosh'd, and bold,
That this our court, infected with their manners,
Shows like a riotous inn. Epicurism and lust
Makes it more like a tavern or a brothel   250
Than a grac'd palace. The shame itself doth speak
For instant remedy. Be then desir'd,
By her that else will take the thing she begs,
A little to disquantity your train,   254
And the remainders that shall still depend
To be such men as may besort your age,
Which know themselves and you.

Lear.   Darkness and devils!
Saddle my horses! call my train together!   258
Degenerate bastard, I'll not trouble thee.
Yet have I left a daughter.

Gon. You strike my people, and your disorder'd rabble
Make servants of their betters.   262

Enter Albany.

Lear. Woe, that too late repents!

                                    «O, sir, are you come?»
Is it your will? Speak, sir.—Prepare my horses.
Ingratitude, thou marble-hearted fiend,

245 should: *and therefore should*
247 disorder'd: *disorderly*   debosh'd: *debauched*
249 Epicurism: *sensuality*
251 grac'd: *gracious*
254 disquantity: *reduce*
255 the remainders: *those remaining*   depend: *be in service*
256 besort: *befit*   263 Woe, that: *woe to him who*

More hideous, when thou show'st thee in a child,   266
Than the sea-monster.
   ⟨*Alb.*   Pray, sir, be patient.⟨
   Lear [*to Goneril*]. Detested kite! thou liest.
My train are men of choice and rarest parts,
That all particulars of duty know,   270
And in the most exact regard support
The worships of their name. O most small fault,
How ugly didst thou in Cordelia show,
Which, like an engine, wrench'd my frame of nature   274
From the fix'd place, drew from my heart all love
And added to the gall. O Lear, Lear, Lear!
Beat at this gate that let thy folly in,
                              [*Striking his head.*]
And thy dear judgment out! Go, go, my people.   278
   Alb. My lord, I am guiltless, as I am ignorant
⟨Of what hath mov'd you⟩.
   Lear.   It may be so, my lord.
Hear, Nature, hear! dear goddess, hear!
Suspend thy purpose, if thou didst intend   282
To make this creature fruitful!
Into her womb convey sterility,
Dry up in her the organs of increase,
And from her derogate body never spring   286
A babe to honor her! If she must teem,
Create her child of spleen, that it may live
And be a thwart, disnatur'd torment to her!

267 sea-monster; *cf. n.*   268 kite: *buzzard*
272 worships: *dignity*
274 engine: *lever*   my frame of nature: *the whole fabric of
    my natural affection*
286 derogate: *degraded*
289 thwart: *perverted*   disnatur'd: *unnatural*

Let it stamp wrinkles in her brow of youth,   290
With cadent tears fret channels in her cheeks,
Turn all her mother's pains and benefits
To laughter and contempt, that she may feel
How sharper than a serpent's tooth it is   294
To have a thankless child! Away, away!   *Exit.*

 Alb. Now, gods that we adore, whereof comes this?

 Gon. Never afflict yourself to know more of it,
But let his disposition have that scope   298
As dotage gives it.

       Enter Lear.

 Lear. What! fifty of my followers at a clap?
Within a fortnight?

 Alb.   What's the matter, sir?

 Lear. I'll tell thee. [*To Goneril.*] Life and death! I am
  asham'd   302
That thou hast power to shake my manhood thus,
That these hot tears, which break from me perforce,
Should make thee worth them. Blasts and fogs upon thee!
Th' untented woundings of a father's curse   306
Pierce every sense about thee! Old fond eyes,
Beweep this cause again, I'll pluck ye out,
And cast you, with the waters that you lose,
To temper clay. «Yea, is it come to this?»   310
⟨Let it be so:⟩ I have another daughter,
Who, I am sure, is kind and comfortable.
When she shall hear this of thee, with her nails

291 cadent: *falling*   298, 299 that scope As; *cf. n.*
300 *Cf. n.*   306 untented: *unsearchable*
308 Beweep: *if you weep for*
310 temper: *soften*   312 comfortable: *comforting*

She'll flay thy wolvish visage. Thou shalt find   314
That I'll resume the shape which thou dost think
I have cast off for ever «thou shalt, I warrant thee».

                    Exit [with Kent and Attendants].

   Gon. Do you mark that?
   Alb. I cannot be so partial, Goneril,   318
To the great love I bear you,—
   Gon. Pray you, content. What, Oswald, ho!
[*To the Fool.*] You, sir, more knave than fool, after your
   master.
   Fool. Nuncle Lear, nuncle Lear! tarry, take thy
fool with thee.   323

> A fox, when one has caught her,
> And such a daughter,
> Should sure to the slaughter,
> If my cap would buy a halter.
> So the fool follows after.

                                        Exit.

⟨*Gon.* This man hath had good counsel. A hundred
   knights!
'Tis politic and safe to let him keep   330
At point a hundred knights! Yes, that on every dream,
Each buzz, each fancy, each complaint, dislike,
He may enguard his dotage with their powers,
And hold our lives in mercy. Oswald, I say!   334
   Alb. Well, you may fear too far.
   Gon.   Safer than trust too far.
Let me still take away the harms I fear,
Not fear still to be taken. I know his heart.
What he hath utter'd I have writ my sister.   338

324–328 Cf. n.   331 At point: *in readiness*
337 taken: *i.e., subjected to harm*

If she sustain him and his hundred knights,
When I have show'd th' unfitness,—>

Enter Steward.

                                    How now, Oswald?
What! have you writ that letter to my sister?
  Osw. Ay, madam.   342
  Gon. Take you some company, and away to horse.
Inform her full of my particular fear,
And thereto add such reasons of your own
As may compact it more. Get you gone,   346
And hasten your return. [*Exit Oswald.*] No, no, my lord,
This milky gentleness and course of yours
Though I condemn not, yet, under pardon,
You are much more atask'd for want of wisdom   350
Than prais'd for harmful mildness.
  Alb. How far your eyes may pierce I cannot tell.
Striving to better, oft we mar what's well.
  Gon. Nay, then—   354
  Alb. Well, well; th' event.   *Exeunt.*

SCENE FIFTH

[*Near Albany's Palace*]

Enter Lear, Kent, and Fool.

  Lear. Go you before to Gloucester with these letters. Acquaint my daughter no further with any-

346 compact: *strengthen*
348 gentleness and course: *gentleness of your course (hendiadys)*
350 atask'd: *blamed; cf. n.*
355 th' event: *the outcome (will show)*   2 Gloucester; *cf. n.*

thing you know than comes from her demand out of the letter. If your diligence be not speedy I shall be there afore you.   5

Kent. I will not sleep, my lord, till I have delivered your letter.   *Exit.*

Fool. If a man's brains were in's heels, were't not in danger of kibes?   9

Lear. Ay, boy.

Fool. Then, I prithee, be merry. Thy wit shall not go slipshod.   12

Lear. Ha, ha, ha!

Fool. Shalt see thy other daughter will use thee kindly; for though she's as like this as a crab's like an apple, yet I can tell what I can tell.   16

Lear. What canst tell, boy?

Fool. She will taste as like this as a crab does to a crab. Thou canst tell why one's nose stands i' th' middle on's face?   20

Lear. No.

Fool. Why, to keep one's eyes of either side's nose, that what a man cannot smell out, he may spy into.   24

Lear. I did her wrong,—

Fool. Canst tell how an oyster makes his shell?

Lear. No.

Fool. Nor I neither; but I can tell why a snail has a house.   29

Lear. Why?

---

9 kibes: *chilblains*
12 slipshod: *in slippers; cf. n.*
15 kindly: *pun, with double meaning of 'gently' and 'naturally'*
    crab: *crabapple*

Fool. Why, to put his head in; not to give it away
to his daughters, and leave his horns without a case.

Lear. I will forget my nature. So kind a father!
Be my horses ready?   34

Fool. Thy asses are gone about 'em. The reason
why the seven stars are no mo than seven is a
pretty reason.   37

Lear. Because they are not eight?

Fool. Yes, indeed. Thou wouldst make a good
fool.

Lear. To take't again perforce! Monster ingratitude!   42

Fool. If thou wert my fool, nuncle, I'd have thee
beaten for being old before thy time.

Lear. How's that?   45

Fool. Thou shouldst not have been old till thou
hadst been wise.

Lear. O let me not be mad, not mad, sweet heaven!
Keep me in temper; I would not be mad!   49

[*Enter Gentleman.*]

How now? Are the horses ready?

Gent. Ready, my lord.

Lear. Come, boy.

Fool. She that's a maid now, and laughs at my departure,   53
Shall not be a maid long, unless things be cut shorter.

                                                Exeunt.

36 the seven stars: *the constellation of the Pleiades*   mo: *more*
49 temper: *mental balance*   S.d. *Cf. n.*   53, 54 *Cf. n.*

ACT SECOND

SCENE FIRST

[Earl of Gloucester's Castle]

Enter Bastard [Edmund] and Curan, meeting.

Edm. Save thee, Curan.

Cur. And you, sir. I have been with your father, and given him notice that the Duke of Cornwall and Regan his duchess will be here with him to-night.   4

Edm. How comes that?

Cur. Nay, I know not. You have heard of the news abroad? I mean the whispered ones, for they are yet but ear-kissing arguments?   8

Edm. Not I. Pray you, what are they?

Cur. Have you heard of no likely wars toward, 'twixt the Dukes of Cornwall and Albany?

Edm. Not a word.   12

Cur. You may do, then, in time. Fare you well, sir.   *Exit.*

Edm. The duke be here to-night! The better! best! This weaves itself perforce into my business.   16
My father hath set guard to take my brother;
And I have one thing, of a queasy question,

Scene First. S.d. *Castle; cf. n.*
1 Save thee: *God save you*   Curan; *cf. n.*
8 ear-kissing arguments: *subjects to be mentioned only with the lips against the ear*
10 toward: *in prospect*   18 queasy question: *hazardous trial*

Which I must act. Briefness and fortune, work!
Brother, a word; descend! Brother, I say!   20

Enter Edgar.

My father watches. O, sir, fly this place!
Intelligence is given where you are hid.
You have now the good advantage of the night.
Have you not spoken 'gainst the Duke of Cornwall?   24
He's coming hither, now, i' th' night, i' th' haste,
And Regan with him. Have you nothing said
Upon his party 'gainst the Duke of Albany?
Advise yourself.

    Edg.   I am sure on't, not a word.   28

    Edm. I hear my father coming. Pardon me;
In cunning I must draw my sword upon you.
Draw; seem to defend yourself. Now quit you well.—
Yield! Come before my father. Light, ho! here!—   32
Fly, brother.—Torches! torches!—So, farewell.

                                 Exit Edgar.

Some blood drawn on me would beget opinion
Of my more fierce endeavor. [*Wounds his arm.*] I have
    seen drunkards
Do more than this in sport. Father! father!   36
Stop! stop! No help?

Enter Gloucester, and Servants with Torches.

    Glo. Now, Edmund, where's the villain?
    Edm. Here stood he in the dark, his sharp sword out,

19 Briefness . . . work; *cf. n.*
27 party: *side*
28 Advise yourself: *think carefully*
31 quit you: *do your part*

Mumbling of wicked charms, conjuring the moon   40
To stand auspicious mistress.
 Glo.   But where is he?
 Edm. Look, sir, I bleed.
 Glo.   Where is the villain, Edmund?
 Edm. Fled this way, sir. When by no means he could—
 Glo. Pursue him, ho! Go after! [*Exeunt some Servants.*]
'By no means' what?   44
 Edm. Persuade me to the murther of your lordship;
But that I told him the revenging gods
'Gainst parricides did all their thunders bend,
Spoke with how manifold and strong a bond   48
The child was bound to th' father. Sir, in fine,
Seeing how loathly opposite I stood
To his unnatural purpose, in fell motion
With his prepared sword he charges home   52
My unprovided body, latch'd mine arm;
But when he saw my best alarum'd spirits,
Bold in the quarrel's right, rous'd to th' encounter,
Or whether gasted by the noise I made,   56
Full suddenly he fled.
 Glo.   Let him fly far.
Not in this land shall he remain uncaught;
And found—dispatch. The noble duke my master,
My worthy arch and patron, comes to-night.   60
By his authority I will proclaim it,
That he which finds him shall deserve our thanks,

40, 41 *Cf. n.*   46 But that; *cf. n.*
48 Spoke: *i.e., and I told him*
51 fell: *fierce*
53 unprovided: *unguarded* latch'd: *caught; cf.n.*
56 gasted: *scared*
59 found—dispatch; *cf. n.*   60 arch: *chief*

Bringing the murderous caitiff to the stake;
He that conceals him, death.   64

   Edm. When I dissuaded him from his intent,
And found him pight to do it, with curst speech
I threaten'd to discover him. He replied:
'Thou unpossessing bastard, dost thou think,   68
If I would stand against thee, would the reposal
Of any trust, virtue, or worth in thee
Make thy words faith'd? No. What I should deny
(As this I would; ay, though thou didst produce   72
My very character), I'd turn it all
To thy suggestion, plot, and damned practice;
And thou must make a dullard of the world,
If they not thought the profits of my death   76
Were very pregnant and potential spurs
To make thee seek it.'

   Glo.   Strong and fasten'd villain!
Would he deny his letter, ⟨said he⟩? «I never got him.»
                             Tucket within.

Hark! the duke's trumpets. I know not why he comes.—
All ports I'll bar. The villain shall not 'scape;   81
The duke must grant me that. Besides, his picture
I will send far and near, that all the kingdom
May have due note of him; and of my land,   84

---

63 caitiff; *cf. n.*   66 pight: *fixed*   curst: *sharp*
67 discover: *expose*
68 unpossessing: *incapable of inheriting*
71 faith'd: *credited*
74 suggestion: *evil prompting*   damned practice: *damnable trickery*
77 pregnant: *inciting*
78 Strong and fasten'd: *gross and hardened*
79 S.d. Tucket: *trumpet-notes, indicating march-signal*
81 ports: *seaports*

Loyal and natural boy, I'll work the means
To make thee capable.

Enter Cornwall, Regan, and Attendants.

Corn. How now, my noble friend! Since I came hither
(Which I can call but now), I have heard strange news.

Reg. If it be true, all vengeance comes too short   89
Which can pursue th' offender. How dost, my lord?

Glo. O, madam, my old heart is crack'd; it's crack'd.

Reg. What! did my father's godson seek your life?   92
He whom my father nam'd? your Edgar?

Glo. O lady, lady, shame would have it hid.

Reg. Was he not companion with the riotous
knights that tended upon my father?   96

Glo. I know not, madam. 'Tis too bad, too bad.

Edm. Yes, madam, he was of that consort.

Reg. No marvel, then, though he were ill affected.
'Tis they have put him on the old man's death,   100
To have th' expense and waste of his revénues.
I have this present evening from my sister
Been well-inform'd of them, and with such cautions
That if they come to sojourn at my house,   104
I'll not be there.

Corn.   Nor I, assure thee, Regan.
Edmund, I hear that you have shown your father
A child-like office.

Edm.   'Twas my duty, sir.

Glo. He did bewray his practice, and receiv'd   108

---

85 natural: *real, my own*   86 capable: *legal heir*
93 *Cf. n.*   98 consort: *company*
101 expense and waste: *wasteful spending; cf. n.*
107 child-like: *filial*   108 bewray: *expose*

This hurt you see, striving to apprehend him.

   Corn. Is he pursu'd?

   Glo.   Ay, my good lord.

   Corn. If he be taken he shall never more

Be fear'd of doing harm. Make your own purpose,   112

How in my strength you please. For you, Edmund,

Whose virtue and obedience doth this instant

So much commend itself, you shall be ours.

Natures of such deep trust we shall much need;   116

You we first seize on.

   Edm.   I shall serve you, sir,

Truly, however else.

   Glo.   For him I thank your Grace.

   Corn. You know not why we came to visit you?

   Reg. Thus out of season threading dark-ey'd night.   120

Occasions, noble Gloucester, of some poise,

Wherein we must have use of your advice.

Our father he hath writ, so hath our sister,

Of differences, which I best thought it fit   124

To answer from our home. The several messengers

From hence attend dispatch. Our good old friend,

Lay comforts to your bosom, and bestow

Your needful counsel to our business,   128

Which craves the instant use.

   Glo.   I serve you, madam.

Your Graces are right welcome.   *Exeunt. Flourish.*

112 of doing: *lest he do*   Make: *execute*
113 How . . . please; *cf. n.*
114 virtue and obedience: *loyal manliness*
116 deep trust: *great fidelity*   121 poise: *weight; cf. n.*
125 from: *away from*   126 From . . . dispatch; *cf. n.*
129 craves . . . use: *must be dealt with at once*

SCENE SECOND

[Courtyard of Gloucester's Castle]

Enter Kent and Steward [Oswald] severally.

Osw. Good dawning to thee, friend. Art of this house?

Kent. Ay.

Osw. Where may we set our horses?   4

Kent. I' th' mire.

Osw. Prithee, if thou lov'st me, tell me.

Kent. I love thee not.

Osw. Why, then I care not for thee.   8

Kent. If I had thee in Lipsbury pinfold, I would make thee care for me.

Osw. Why dost thou use me thus? I know thee not.   12

Kent. Fellow, I know thee.

Osw. What dost thou know me for?

Kent. A knave, a rascal, an eater of broken meats; a base, proud, shallow, beggarly, three-suited, hundred-pound, filthy, worsted-stocking knave; a lily-liver'd, action-taking knave; a whoreson, glass-gazing, superserviceable, finical rogue; one-trunk-inheriting

Scene Second. S.d. severally: *entering at different doors; cf. n.*
1 Art . . . house: *are you employed here?*
7 I love thee not; *cf. n.*   9 Lipsbury pinfold; *cf. n.*
15 broken meats: *scraps*   16 three-suited; *cf. n.*
18 action-taking: *given to lawsuits*   glass-gazing: *fond of the*
                                                          mirror
19 superserviceable: *officious*   one-trunk-inheriting: *born to*
                                                          practically nothing

slave; one that wouldst be a bawd, in way of good
service, and art nothing but the composition of a
knave, beggar, coward, pandar, and the son and heir
of a mongrel bitch: one whom I will beat into clam-
orous whining if thou deniest the least syllable of
thy addition.   25

Osw. Why, what a monstrous fellow art thou,
thus to rail on one that is neither known of thee nor
knows thee!   28

Kent. What a brazen-faced varlet art thou, to deny
thou knowest me! Is it two days since I tripped up
thy heels and beat thee before the king? Draw, you
rogue; for, though it be night, yet the moon shines:
I'll make a sop o' th' moonshine of you. [*Drawing
his sword.*] «Draw,» you whoreson, cullionly barber-
monger, draw.   35

Osw. Away! I have nothing to do with thee.

Kent. Draw, you rascal! You come with letters
against the king, and take Vanity the puppet's part
against the royalty of her father. Draw, you rogue,
or I'll so carbonado your shanks! Draw, you rascal!
come your ways!

Osw. Help, ho! Murther! Help!   42

Kent. Strike, you slave! Stand, rogue, stand! You
neat slave, strike!   [*Beating him.*]

Osw. Help, ho! Murther! murther!

---

33 sop o' th' moonshine: *make moonlight shine through you;
cf. n.*
34 cullionly: *knavish*   barber-monger: *patron of the barber's
shop*
38 Vanity the puppet's: *Vanity, a personified character in the
Interludes (Goneril is meant)*   40 carbonado: *slice*
41 your ways: *along (with me)*   44 neat: *over-dressed*

Enter Edmund with his rapier drawn, Gloucester,
the Duke and Duchess, Servants.

Edm. How now! What's the matter! ⟨Part!⟩   46

Kent. With you, goodman boy, if you please! Come,
I'll flesh ye! Come on, young master.

Glo. Weapons? arms? What's the matter here?

Corn. Keep peace, upon your lives.   50
He dies that strikes again. What is the matter?

Reg. The messengers from our sister and the king!

Corn. What is your difference? Speak.

Osw. I am scarce in breath, my lord.   54

Kent. No marvel, you have so bestirred your valor.
You cowardly rascal, nature disclaims in thee. A
tailor made thee.

Corn. Thou art a strange fellow. A tailor make a
man?   59

Kent. «Ay» a tailor, sir. A stone-cutter or a painter
could not have made him so ill, though they had been
but two hours o' th' trade.   62

Corn. Speak yet, how grew your quarrel?

Osw. This ancient ruffian, sir, whose life I have
spar'd at suit of his grey beard,—   65

Kent. Thou whoreson zed! thou unnecessary letter! My lord, if you will give me leave, I will tread
this unbolted villain into mortar, and daub the
wall of a jakes with him. Spare my grey beard, you
wagtail!   70

46 Part: *separate yourselves*
47 With you; *cf. n.*   goodman: *a plebeian form of address*
56 disclaims: *claims no share*
63 yet: *however*   66 zed; *cf. n.*
68 unbolted: *unrefined*   69 a jakes: *a privy*
70 wagtail: *a nervous and impudent small bird*

Corn. Peace, sirrah!
You beastly knave, know you no reverence?

    Kent. Yes, sir; but anger hath a privilege.

    Corn. Why art thou angry?   74

    Kent. That such a slave as this should wear a sword,
Who wears no honesty. Such smiling rogues as these,
Like rats, oft bite the holy cords a-twain
Which are too intrinse t'unloose; smooth every passion 78
That in the natures of their lords rebel,
Bring oil to fire, snow to their colder moods;
Renege, affirm, and turn their halcyon beaks
With every gale and vary of their masters,   82
Knowing nought, like dogs, but following.
A plague upon your epileptic visage!
Smoil you my speeches, as I were a fool?
Goose, if I had you upon Sarum plain,   86
I'd drive ye cackling home to Camelot.

    Corn. What! art thou mad, old fellow?

    Glo. How fell you out? say that.

    Kent. No cóntraries hold more antipathy   90
Than I and such a knave.

    Corn. Why dost thou call him knave? What is his fault?

    Kent. His countenance likes me not.

    Corn. No more, perchance, does mine, nor his, nor
hers.   95

    Kent. Sir, 'tis my occupation to be plain.
I have seen better faces in my time

77, 78 holy cords . . . too intrinse; *cf. n.*
78 smooth: *make the way easy for*
81 Renege: *deny*   halcyon; *cf. n.*
82 gale: *breeze*   vary: *vacillation*
85 Smoil; *cf. n.*   86 Sarum: *Salisbury*
87 Camelot; *cf. n.*   97 better faces; *cf. n.*

Than stands on any shoulder that I see   98
Before me at this instant.
   Corn.   This is some fellow,
Who, having been prais'd for bluntness, doth affect
A saucy roughness, and constrains the garb
Quite from his nature. He cannot flatter, he.   102
An honest mind and plain, he must speak truth.
An they will take it, so; if not, he's plain.
These kind of knaves I know, which in this plainness
Harbor more craft and more corrupter ends   106
Than twenty silly-ducking óbservants,
That stretch their duties nicely.
   Kent. Sir, in good faith, in síncere verity,
Under th' allowance of your great aspéct,   110
Whose influence, like the wreath of radiant fire
Flickering on Phœbus' front,—
   Corn.   What mean'st by this?
   Kent. To go out of my dialect, which you discom-
mend so much. I know, sir, I am no flatterer. He that
beguiled you in a plain accent was a plain knave;
which for my part I will not be, though I should win
your displeasure to entreat me to 't.   117
   Corn. What was th' offence you gave him?
   Osw. I never gave him any.
It pleas'd the king his master very late
To strike at me upon his misconstruction;   121

101 constrains the garb: *forces the fashion*
102 from: *contrary to*
104 he's plain: *he forces it on them anyway*
107 óbservants: *courtiers*   108 nicely: *fastidiously*
112 Flickering on; *cf. n.*   front: *forehead*
117 your displeasure; *cf. n.*
121 upon his misconstruction: *having misconstrued my conduct*

When he, conjunct, and flattering his displeasure,
Tripp'd me behind; being down, insulted, rail'd,
And put upon him such a deal of man,
That worthied him, got praises of the king   125
For him attempting who was self-subdu'd;
And, in the fleshment of this dread exploit,
Drew on me here again.

  Kent.   None of these rogues and cowards
But Ajax is their fool.

  Corn.   Fetch forth the stocks!   129
You stubborn ancient knave, you reverent braggart,
We'll teach you.

  Kent.   Sir, I am too old to learn.
Call not your stocks for me. I serve the king,
On whose employment I was sent to you.   133
You shall do small respects, show too bold malice
Against the grace and person of my master,
Stocking his messenger.

  Corn. Fetch forth the stocks! As I have life and honor,
There shall he sit till noon.   138

  Reg. Till noon! Till night, my lord, and all night too.

  Kent. Why, madam, if I were your father's dog,
You should not use me so.

  Reg.   Sir, being his knave, I will.   141

  Corn. This is a fellow of the self-same color

---

22 conjunct: *in league*
23 being down, insulted: *I being down, he exulted*
25 worthied: *covered with dignity*
27 in . . . of: *to feed the appetite created by*
29 Ajax; *cf. n.*
30 reverent: *for 'reverend' (old enough to know better)*
34 small respects: *little in the way of compliment (ironic)*
36 Stocking; *cf. n.*

Our sister speaks of. Come, bring away the stocks.

Stocks brought out.

   Glo. Let me beseech your Grace not to do so.

«His fault is much, and the good king his master   145
Will check him for't. Your purpos'd low correction
Is such as vilest and contemned'st wretches
For pilferings and most common trespasses
Are punish'd with.» The king ⟨his master needs⟩ must take it ill,   149
That he's so slightly valu'd in his messenger,
Should have him thus restrain'd.

   Corn.   I'll answer that.

   Reg. My sister may receive it much more worse
To have her gentleman abus'd, assaulted,   153
«For following her affairs. Put in his legs.»

[Kent is put in the stocks.]

Come, my good lord, away.

Exit [with all but Gloucester and Kent].

   Glo. I am sorry for thee, friend. 'Tis the duke's pleasure,
Whose disposition, all the world well knows,   157
Will not be rubb'd nor stopp'd. I'll entreat for thee.

   Kent. Pray, do not, sir. I have watch'd and travell'd hard.
Some time I shall sleep out, the rest I'll whistle.
A good man's fortune may grow out at heels.   161
Give you good morrow!

   Glo. The duke's to blame in this. 'Twill be ill taken.

Exit

   Kent. Good king, that must approve the common saw

---

146 check: *reprimand*   147 vilest and contemned'st; *cf. n*
150, 151 *Cf. n.*
159 watch'd: *lost sleep*   158 rubb'd: *checked*
                            164 approve: *illustrat*

Thou out of heaven's benediction com'st   165
To the warm sun.
Approach, thou beacon to this under globe,
That by thy comfortable beams I may
Peruse this letter. Nothing almost sees miracles   169
But misery. I know 'tis from Cordelia,
Who hath most fortunately been inform'd
Of my obscured course.
[Reads] . . .

> And shall find time
> From this enormous state, seeking to give   174
> Losses their remedies.

All weary and o'er-watch'd!
Take vantage, heavy eyes, not to behold
This shameful lodging.   178
Fortune, good night. Smile once more; turn thy wheel!
                                        Sleeps.

[SCENE THIRD]

Enter Edgar.

Edg. I heard myself proclaim'd,
And by the happy hollow of a tree
Escap'd the hunt. No port is free; no place,
That guard and most unusual vigilance   4
Does not attend my taking. Whiles I may 'scape

165 heaven's benediction; cf. n.
169, 170 Nothing . . . misery; cf. n.
173–175 And . . . remedies; cf. n.
177 Take vantage: use the opportunity (which sleep offers)
Scene Third; cf. n.

I will preserve myself, and am bethought
To take the basest and most poorest shape
Which the impetuous blasts, with eyeless rage,   8
Brought near to beast. My face I'll grime with filth,
Blanket my loins, elf all my hair in knots,
And with presented nakedness outface
The winds and persecutions of the sky.   12
The country gives me proof and precedent
Of Bedlam beggars, who with roaring voices
Strike in their numb'd and mortified bare arms
Pins, wooden pricks, nails, sprigs of rosemary;   16
And with this horrible object from low farms,
Poor pelting villages, sheep-cotes, and mills,
Sometime with lunatic bans, sometime with prayers,
Enforce their charity. Poor Turlygod! poor Tom!   20
That's something yet. Edgar I nothing am.   *Exit.*

[SCENE FOURTH

Courtyard of Gloucester's Castle]

Enter Lear, Fool, and Gentleman.

   Lear. 'Tis strange that they should so depart from home,
And not send back my messenger.
   Gent.   As I learn'd,
The night before there was no purpose in them
Of this remove.

10 elf: *twist*   14 Bedlam beggars; *cf. n*
17 object; *spectacle*   18 pelting: *contemptible*
19 bans: *curses*   20 Turlygod . . . Tom; *cf. n*
21 Edgar I nothing am: *as Edgar I am nothing*

Kent.   Hail to thee, noble master!   4
Lear. Ha!
Mak'st thou this shame thy pastime?
Kent.   ⟨No, my lord.⟩
     Fool. Ha, ha! he wears cruel garters. Horses are
tied by the head, dogs and bears by th' neck, monkeys
by th' loins, and men by th' legs: when a man's
over-lusty at legs, then he wears wooden nether-
stocks.
     Lear. What's he that hath so much thy place mis-
          took   12
To set thee here?
Kent.   It is both he and she,
Your son and daughter.
     Lear. No.
     Kent. Yes.   16
     Lear. No, I say.
     Kent. I say, yea.
     «*Lear.* No, no; they would not.
     Kent. Yes, they have.»   20
     Lear. By Jupiter, I swear, no.
     ⟨*Kent.* By Juno, I swear, ay.
     Lear.⟩   They durst not do't;
They could not, would not do't. 'Tis worse than murther
To do upon respect such violent outrage.   24
Resolve me, with all modest haste, which way
Thou mightst deserve, or they impose, this usage,
Coming from us.
     Kent.   My lord, when at their home

---

7 cruel: *pun on crewel; i.e., worsted*
10 nether-stocks: *stockings*   24 *Cf. n.*
25 Resolve: *inform*   27 Coming: *considering that you came*

I did commend your highness' letters to them,   28
Ere I was risen from the place that show'd
My duty kneeling, there came a reeking post,
Stew'd in his haste, half breathless, panting forth
From Goneril his mistress salutations;   32
Deliver'd letters, spite of intermission,
Which presently they read. On whose contents
They summon'd up their meiny, straight took horse;
Commanded me to follow and attend   36
The leisure of their answer, gave me cold looks.
And meeting here the other messenger,
Whose welcome, I perceiv'd, had poison'd mine—
Being the very fellow which of late   40
Display'd so saucily against your highness—
Having more man than wit about me, drew.
He rais'd the house with loud and coward cries.
Your son and daughter found this trespass worth   44
The shame which here it suffers.
    ⟨*Fool*. Winter's not gone yet, if the wild geese fly
    that way.

> Fathers that wear rags   48
>   Do make their children blind,
> But fathers that bear bags
>   Shall see their children kind.
> Fortune, that arrant whore,   52
> Ne'er turns the key to th' poor.

But for all this thou shalt have as many dolors for
thy daughters as thou canst tell in a year.⟩

33 spite of intermission: *making no bones of interrupting me*
34 On: *on perceiving*   35 meiny: *retinue of attendants*
38–42 And . . . drew; *cf. n.*   49 blind: *i.e., to filial duty*
53 turns the key: *unlocks the door*
54 dolors: *pun on dollars*   55 tell: *count; also 'narrate'*

Lear. O how this mother swells up toward my heart! 56
Hysterica passio! Down, thou climbing sorrow!
Thy element's below. Where is this daughter?

Kent. With the earl, sir: here within.

Lear [*to Attendants*]. Follow me not. Stay here.   *Exit.*

   Gent. Made you no more offence than what you
speak of?

Kent. None.

How chance the king comes with so small a number? 64

   Fool. An thou hadst been set i' th' stocks for that
question, thou'dst well deserved it.

   Kent. Why, fool?   67

   Fool. We'll set thee to school to an ant, to teach
thee there's no laboring i' th' winter. All that follow
their noses are led by their eyes but blind men; and
there's not a nose among twenty but can smell him
that's stinking. Let go thy hold when a great wheel
runs down a hill, lest it break thy neck with following; but the great one that goes upward, let him
draw thee after. When a wise man gives thee better
counsel, give me mine again. I would have none but
knaves follow it, since a fool gives it.   77

       That sir which serves and seeks for gain,
          And follows but for form,
       Will pack when it begins to rain,
          And leave thee in the storm.
       But I will tarry, the fool will stay,
          And let the wise man fly:
       The knave turns fool that runs away;
          The fool no knave, perdy.

56 mother: *vertigo*
56, 57 mother . . . *Hysterica passio; cf. n.*
76 none but knaves; *cf. n.*
80 pack: *hurry off*   85 perdy: *by God, pardieu*

Kent. Where learn'd you this, fool?
Fool. Not i' th' stocks, fool.   87

Enter Lear and Gloucester.

Lear. Deny to speak with me! They are sick! They are
    weary!
They have travell'd all the night! Mere fetches,
The images of revolt and flying off.
Fetch me a better answer.
    Glo.   My dear lord,
You know the fiery quality of the duke;   92
How unremovable and fix'd he is
In his own course.
    Lear. Vengeance! plague! death! confusion!
What fiery quality? Why, Gloucester, Gloucester!   96
I'd speak with the Duke of Cornwall and his wife.
⟨*Glo.* Well, my good lord, I have inform'd them so.
    Lear. Inform'd them! Dost thou understand me, man?⟩
    Glo. Ay, my good lord.   100
    Lear. The king would speak with Cornwall; the dear
        father
Would with his daughter speak, commands her service.
⟨Are they inform'd of this? My breath and blood!⟩
Fiery duke! Tell the hot duke that Lear—   104
No, but not yet; may be he is not well.
Infirmity doth still neglect all office
Whereto our health is bound. We are not ourselves
When nature, being oppress'd, commands the mind   108
To suffer with the body. I'll forbear;

88 Deny: *refuse*
89 fetches: *tricks*   90 flying off: *desertion*
102, 104 Cf. *n.*   106 office: *duty*

And am fall'n out with my more headier will,
To take the indispos'd and sickly fit
For the sound man. Death on my state! [*Looking on
    Kent.*] Wherefore   112
Should he sit here? This act persuades me
That this remotion of the duke and her
Is practice only. Give me my servant forth.
Go tell the duke and's wife I'd speak with them,   116
Now, presently. Bid them come forth and hear me,
Or at their chamber-door I'll beat the drum
Till it cry sleep to death.   119
    Glo. I would have all well betwixt you.   *Exit.*
    Lear. O, me! my heart, my rising heart! but, down!
    Fool. Cry to it, nuncle, as the cockney did to the
eels when she put 'em i' th' paste alive. She knapped
'em o' th' coxcombs with a stick, and cried, 'Down,
wantons, down!' 'Twas her brother that, in pure
kindness to his horse, buttered his hay.   126

    Enter Cornwall, Regan, Gloucester, Servants.

    Lear. Good morrow to you both.
    Corn.   Hail to your Grace.
                      Kent here set at liberty.
    Reg. I am glad to see your highness.   128
    Lear. Regan, I think you are. I know what reason
I have to think so. If thou shouldst not be glad,
I would divorce me from thy mother's tomb,
Sepúlchring an adult'ress.—[*To Kent.*] O! are you free?

110 more headier: *too headstrong*   114 remotion: *removal*
119 cry sleep to death: *murder sleep*
122 cockney: *city woman*
123 paste: *pie-dough*   knapped: *rapped*
132 Sepúlchring: *for enclosing*

Some other time for that. Beloved Regan,   133
Thy sister's naught. O Regan! she hath tied
Sharp-tooth'd unkindness, like a vulture, here.

                              [*Points to his heart.*]

I can scarce speak to thee—thou'lt not believe—   136
Of how deprav'd a quality—O Regan!

   Reg. I pray you, sir, take patience. I have hope
You less know how to value her desert
Than she to scant her duty.

⟨*Lear.*   Say, how is that?   140

   Reg. I cannot think my sister in the least
Would fail her obligation. If, sir, perchance
She have restrain'd the riots of your followers,
'Tis on such ground and to such wholesome end   144
As clears her from all blame.⟩

   Lear. My curses on her!

   Reg.   O, sir, you are old.
Nature in you stands on the very verge
Of her confíne. You should be rul'd and led   148
By some discretion that discerns your state
Better than you yourself. Therefore I pray you
That to our sister you do make return.
Say, you have wrong'd her, sir.

   Lear.   Ask her forgiveness?   152
Do you but mark how this becomes the house:
'Dear daughter, I confess that I am old.
Age is unnecessary: on my knees I beg
That you'll vouchsafe me raiment, bed, and food.'   156

   Reg. Good sir, no more; these are unsightly tricks.

---

134 naught: *worthless*   137 quality: *manner*
140 scant; *cf. n.*   147, 148 on . . . confine; *cf. n.*
148 confíne: *territory*   153 the house: *our exalted family*

Return you to my sister.

    Lear.   Never, Regan.

She hath abated me of half my train,

Look'd black upon me, struck me with her tongue,   160

Most serpent-like, upon the very heart.

All the stor'd vengeances of heaven fall

On her ingrateful top! Strike her young bones,

You taking airs, with lameness!

    Corn.   Fie, sir, fie!   164

    Lear. You nimble lightnings, dart your blinding flames

Into her scornful eyes! Infect her beauty,

You fen-suck'd fogs, drawn by the powerful sun,

To fall and blast her pride!   168

    Reg. O the blest gods! So will you wish on me,

When the rash mood is on.

    Lear. No, Regan, thou shalt never have my curse.

Thy tender-hefted nature shall not give   172

Thee o'er to harshness. Her eyes are fierce, but thine

Do comfort and not burn. 'Tis not in thee

To grudge my pleasures, to cut off my train,

To bandy hasty words, to scant my sizes,   176

And, in conclusion, to oppose the bolt

Against my coming in. Thou better know'st

The offices of nature, bond of childhood,

Effects of courtesy, dues of gratitude;   180

Thy half o' th' kingdom hast thou not forgot,

Wherein I thee endow'd.

    Reg.   Good sir, to th' purpose.

---

159 She . . . train; *cf. n.*   abated: *deprived*
164 taking: *possessing, in the sense of malignant*
168 fall: *make fall*
172 tender-hefted: *sensitive; cf. n.*   176 sizes: *allowances*

Lear. Who put my man i' th' stocks?

                               Tucket within.

   Corn.   What trumpet's that?

   Reg. I know 't: my sister's. This approves her letter, 184
That she would soon be here.

              Enter Steward [Oswald].

                     Is your lady come?

   Lear. This is a slave, whose easy-borrow'd pride
Dwells in the fickle grace of her 'a follows.
Out, varlet, from my sight!

   Corn.   What means your Grace? 188

   Lear. Who stock'd my servant? Regan, I have good hope
Thou didst not know on 't.

                Enter Goneril.

             Who comes here? O heavens,
If you do love old men, if your sweet sway
Allow obedience, if you yourselves are old,   192
Make it your cause. Send down and take my part!
[*To Goneril.*] Art not asham'd to look upon this beard?
O Regan, will you take her by the hand?

   Gon. Why not by th' hand, sir? How have I offended?
All's not offence that indiscretion finds   197
And dotage terms so.

   Lear.   O sides, you are too tough!
Will you yet hold?—How came my man i' th' stocks?

   Corn. I set him there, sir; but his own disorders   200
Deserv'd much less advancement.

   Lear.   You? Did you?

187 'a: *he*   192 Allow: *commend (as an example)*
200 disorders: *disorderly acts*

Reg. I pray you, father, being weak, seem so.
If till the expiration of your month
You will return and sojourn with my sister,   204
Dismissing half your train, come then to me.
I am now from home, and out of that provision
Which shall be needful for your entertainment.

    Lear. Return to her? and fifty men dismiss'd!   208
No, rather I abjure all roofs, and choose
To wage against the enmity o' th' air,
To be a comrade with the wolf and owl:
Necessity's sharp pinch! Return with her?   212
Why, the hot-blooded France, that dowerless took
Our youngest born, I could as well be brought
To knee his throne, and, squire-like, pension beg
To keep base life afoot. Return with her?   216
Persuade me rather to be slave and sumpter
To this detested groom.

    Gon.   At your choice, sir.

    Lear. I prithee, daughter, do not make me mad.
I will not trouble thee, my child. Farewell.   220
We'll no more meet, no more see one another;
But yet thou art my flesh, my blood, my daughter,—
Or rather a disease that's in my flesh,
Which I must needs call mine. Thou art a bile,   224
A plague-sore, an embossed carbuncle,
In my corrupted blood. But I'll not chide thee.
Let shame come when it will, I do not call it.
I do not bid the thunder-bearer shoot,   228
Nor tell tales of thee to high-judging Jove.

---

210 wage: *wage war*   217 sumpter: *packhorse (or its driver)*
218 groom: *i.e., Oswald*
224 bile: *boil; cf. n.*   225 embossed: *swollen*

Mend when thou canst; be better at thy leisure.
I can be patient; I can stay with Regan,
I and my hundred knights.

    Reg.   Not altogether so.   232
I look'd not for you yet, nor am provided
For your fit welcome. Give ear, sir, to my sister;
For those that mingle reason with your passion
Must be content to think you old, and so—   236
But she knows what she does.

    Lear.   Is this well spoken?
    Reg. I dare avouch it, sir. What! fifty followers?
Is it not well? What should you need of more?
Yea, or so many, sith that both charge and danger   240
Speak 'gainst so great a number? How, in one house,
Should many people under two commands
Hold amity? 'Tis hard; almost impossible.

    Gon. Why might not you, my lord, receive attendance
From those that she calls servants, or from mine?   245

    Reg. Why not, my lord? If then they chanc'd to slack ye,
We could control them. If you will come to me
(For now I spy a danger), I entreat you   248
To bring but five-and-twenty. To no more
Will I give place or notice.

    Lear. I gave you all—
    Reg.   And in good time you gave it.
    Lear. Made you my guardians, my depositaries,   252
But kept a reservation to be follow'd
With such a number. What! must I come to you
With five-and-twenty? Regan, said you so?

235 mingle . . . passion; *cf. n.*
239 Is it not well: *is not that enough?*
250 notice: *countenance*   252 depositaries: *trustees*

Reg. And speak't again, my lord. No more with me.

   Lear. Those wicked creatures yet do look well-favor'd,
When others are more wicked; not being the worst
Stands in some rank of praise. [*To Goneril.*] I'll go with
   thee.
Thy fifty yet doth double five-and-twenty,   260
And thou art twice her love.

   Gon.   Hear me, my lord.
What need you five-and-twenty? ten? or five?
To follow in a house, where twice so many
Have a command to tend you?

   Reg.   What need one?   264

   Lear. O reason not the need! Our basest beggars
Are in the poorest thing superfluous.
Allow not nature more than nature needs,
Man's life is cheap as beast's. Thou art a lady.   268
If only to go warm were gorgeous,
Why, nature needs not what thou gorgeous wear'st,
Which scarcely keeps thee warm. But for true need,—
You heavens, give me that patience, patience I need!   272
You see me here, you gods, a poor old man,
As full of grief as age, wretched in both!
If it be you that stirs these daughters' hearts
Against their father, fool me not so much   276
To bear it tamely. Touch me with noble anger,
And let not women's weapons, water-drops,
Stain my man's cheeks! No, you unnatural hags,
I will have such revenges on you both   280

266 in: *i.e., in possessing*   superfluous: *possessed of more
                                than they need*
268–271 Thou . . . warm; *cf. n.*
276 fool . . . much: *make me not such a fool*

That all the world shall—I will do such things,—
What they are yet I know not,—but they shall be
The terrors of the earth. You think I'll weep?
No, I'll not weep.   284
I have full cause of weeping, but this heart

                              Storm and Tempest.
Shall break into a hundred thousand flaws
Or ere I'll weep. O, fool, I shall go mad.

                    Exeunt Lear, Gloucester, Kent, and Fool.
    Corn. Let us withdraw. 'Twill be a storm.   288
    Reg. This house is little. The old man and his people
Cannot be well bestow'd.
    Gon. 'Tis his own blame; hath put himself from rest,
And must needs taste his folly.   292
    Reg. For his particular, I'll receive him gladly,
But not one follower.
    Gon.   So am I purpos'd.
Where is my Lord of Gloucester?
    Corn. Follow'd the old man forth. He is return'd.   296

                        Enter Gloucester.

    Glo. The king is in high rage.
    ⟨*Corn.*   Whither is he going?
    Glo. He calls to horse; but⟩ will I know not whither.
    Corn. 'Tis best to give him way; he leads himself.
    Gon. My lord, entreat him by no means to stay.   300
    Glo. Alack! the night comes on, and the bleak winds
Do sorely ruffle. For many miles about
There's scarce a bush.

286 flaws: *pieces*
293 For his particular: *in regard to himself*   294–296 Cf. *n.*
301 bleak; *cf. n.*   302 ruffle: *bluster*

Reg.   O, sir, to wilful men,
The injuries that they themselves procure   304
Must be their schoolmasters. Shut up your doors.
He is attended with a desperate train,
And what they may incense him to, being apt
To have his ear abus'd, wisdom bids fear.   308
    Corn. Shut up your doors, my lord; 'tis a wild night.
My Regan counsels well. Come out o' th' storm.   *Exeunt.*

ACT THIRD

SCENE FIRST

[The Heath]

Storm still. Enter Kent and a Gentleman at several doors.

    Kent. Who's there, besides foul weather?
    Gent. One minded like the weather, most unquietly.
    Kent. I know you. Where's the king?
    Gent. Contending with the fretful elements;   4
Bids the wind blow the earth into the sea,
Or swell the curled waters 'bove the main,
That things might change or cease. «Tears his white hair,
Which the impetuous blasts, with eyeless rage,   8
Catch in their fury and make nothing of;
Strives in his little world of man t'out-scorn
The to-and-fro-conflicting wind and rain.

307 apt: *naturally disposed*   310 storm; *cf. n.*
6 main: *land*   10 little world of man: *microcosm; cf. n.*

This night, wherein the cub-drawn bear would couch, 12
The lion and the belly-pinched wolf
Keep their fur dry, unbonneted he runs,
And bids what will take all.»

    Kent.   But who is with him?

    Gent. None but the fool, who labors to out-jest 16
His heart-struck injuries.

    Kent.   Sir, I do know you;
And dare, upon the warrant of my note,
Commend a dear thing to you. There is division,
(Although as yet the face of it is cover'd 20
With mutual cunning) 'twixt Albany and Cornwall,
⟨Who have—as who have not, that their great stars
Thron'd and set high—servants, who seem no less,
Which are to France the spies and speculations 24
Intelligent of our state. What hath been seen,
Either in snuffs and packings of the dukes,
Or the hard rein which both of them have borne
Against the old kind king, or something deeper, 28
Whereof perchance these are but furnishings–⟩
«But, true it is, from France there comes a power
Into this scatter'd kingdom; who already,
Wise in our negligence, have secret feet 32
In some of our best ports, and are at point
To show their open banner. Now to you:
If in my credit you dare build so far

12 cub-drawn: *dry-sucked, ravenous*
14 unbonneted: *without a hat*   18 note: *observation*
23 no less: *no less than true servants*
24 speculations: *scouts*   25 Intelligent: *giving intelligence*
26 snuffs: *resentments*   packings: *hidden plots*
29 furnishings: *outer coverings; cf. n.*
31 scatter'd: *disunited*

To make your speed to Dover, you shall find   36
Some that will thank you, making just report
Of how unnatural and bemadding sorrow
The king hath cause to plain.
I am a gentleman of blood and breeding,   40
And from some knowledge and assurance offer
This office to you.»
   Gent. I will talk further with you.
   Kent.   No, do not.
For confirmation that I am much more   44
Than my out-wall, open this purse and take
What it contains. If you shall see Cordelia
(As fear not but you shall), show her this ring,
And she will tell you who your fellow is   48
That yet you do not know. Fie on this storm!
I will go seek the king.
   Gent. Give me your hand. Have you no more to say?
   Kent. Few words, but, to effect, more than all yet: 52
That when we have found the king,—in which your pain
That way, I'll this,—he that first lights on him
Holla the other.   *Exeunt.*

37 making: *for making*   39 plain: *complain*
41 knowledge and assurance: *sure knowledge*
45 my out-wall: *the servant livery I wear*
48 fellow: *companion*   52 to effect: *in importance*

SCENE SECOND

[Another part of the Heath]

Storm still. Enter Lear and Fool.

Lear. Blow, winds, and crack your cheeks! rage! blow!
You cataracts and hurricanoes, spout
Till you have drench'd the steeples, drown'd the cocks!
You sulphurous and thought-executing fires,   4
Vaunt-couriers of oak-cleaving thunderbolts,
Singe my white head! And thou, all-shaking thunder,
Strike flat the thick rotundity o' th' world!
Crack nature's moulds, all germens spill at once   8
That make ingrateful man!

    Fool. O nuncle, court holy-water in a dry house is
    better than this rain-water out o' door. Good nuncle,
    in; ask thy daughters' blessing. Here's a night pities
    neither wise men nor fools.

    Lear. Rumble thy bellyful! Spit fire! spout rain!   14
Nor rain, wind, thunder, fire, are my daughters.
I tax not you, you elements, with unkindness;
I never gave you kingdom, call'd you children,
You owe me no subscription. Then, let fall
Your horrible pleasure. Here I stand, your slave,
A poor, infirm, weak, and despis'd old man.   20
But yet I call you servile ministers,

2 hurricanoes: *water-spouts*
3 cocks: *weathercocks on steeples*
4 thought-executing: *acting Jove's thought*
5 Vaunt-couriers: *advance messengers*   8 germens: *seeds*
10 court holy-water: *flattery*   18 subscription: *allegiance*

That will with two pernicious daughters join
Your high-engender'd battles 'gainst a head
So old and white as this. O! O! 'tis foul.   24

    Fool. He that has a house to put's head in has a
good head-piece.

> The codpiece that will house
>   Before the head has any,   28
> The head and he shall louse;
>   So beggars marry many.
> The man that makes his toe
>   What he his heart should make,   32
> Shall of a corn cry woe,
>   And turn his sleep to wake.

For there was never yet fair woman but she made
mouths in a glass.   36
    Lear. No, I will be the pattern of all patience.
I will say nothing.

Enter Kent.

    Kent. Who's there?
    Fool. Marry, here's grace and a codpiece; that's a
wise man and a fool.   41
    Kent. Alas, sir, are you here? Things that love night
Love not such nights as these. The wrathful skies
Gallow the very wanderers of the dark,   44
And make them keep their caves. Since I was man
Such sheets of fire, such bursts of horrid thunder,
Such groans of roaring wind and rain, I never

23 high-engender'd battles; *cf. n.*
27 cod-piece: *part of man's dress between the legs*
30 Cf. *n.*   31, 32 toe, heart; *cf. n.*
40 grace: *majesty*   44 Gallow: *terrify*

Remember to have heard. Man's nature cannot carry   48
Th' affliction nor the fear.

   Lear.   Let the great gods,
That keep this dreadful pudder o'er our heads,
Find out their enemies now. Tremble, thou wretch,
That hast within thee undivulged crimes   52
Unwhipp'd of justice; hide thee, thou bloody hand,
Thou perjur'd, and thou simular of virtue
That art incestuous. Caitiff, to pieces shake,
That under covert and convenient seeming   56
Hast practis'd on man's life. Close pent-up guilts,
Rive your concealing continents, and cry
These dreadful summoners grace. I am a man
More sinn'd against than sinning.

   Kent.   Alack! bare-headed!
Gracious my lord, hard by here is a hovel.   61
Some friendship will it lend you 'gainst the tempest.
Repose you there while I to this hard house
(More harder than the stones whereof 'tis rais'd,   64
Which even but now, demanding after you,
Denied me to come in) return and force
Their scanted courtesy.

   Lear.   My wits begin to turn.
Come on, my boy. How dost, my boy? Art cold?   68
I am cold myself. Where is this straw, my fellow?
The art of our necessities is strange,
That can make vile things precious. Come, your hovel.
Poor fool and knave, I have one part in my heart   72
That's sorry yet for thee.

---

50 pudder: *'powther'* (*Q*), *uproar*   54 simular: *simulator*
58 Rive: *split*   continents: *covers*
59 grace: *mercy*   71 vile; *cf. n.*

Fool.

> He that has and-a little tiny wit,
>> With hey, ho, the wind and the rain,
> Must make content with his fortunes fit,
>> Though the rain it raineth every day.

Lear. True, my good boy. Come, bring us to this hovel.

Exit [with Kent].

⟨*Fool.* This is a brave night to cool a courtesan.
I'll speak a prophecy cre I go: 　　　　　　　　　80

> When priests are more in word than matter;
> When brewers mar their malt with water;
> When nobles are their tailors' tutors;
> No heretics burn'd but wenches' suitors; 　　84
> When every case in law is right,
> No squire in debt, nor no poor knight;
> When slanders do not live in tongues;
> Nor cutpurses come not to throngs; 　　　88
> When usurers tell their gold i' th' field,
> And bawds and whores do churches build:
> Then shall the realm of Albion
> Come to great confusion. 　　　　　　92
> Then comes the time, who lives to see't,
> That going shall be us'd with feet.

This prophecy Merlin shall make, for I live before his time.

Exit.⟩

76 Cf. *n.*　　　　　　　　　　　79–96 Cf. *n.*
83 Cf. *n.*　　　　　　　84 No . . . suitors; cf. *n.*
86 nor no poor knight; cf. *n.*
93, 94 Then . . . feet; cf. *n.*　　　　95 Merlin; cf. *n.*

SCENE THIRD

[Gloucester's Castle]

Enter Gloucester and the Bastard, with lights.

Glo. Alack, alack, Edmund! I like not this unnatural dealing. When I desired their leave that I might pity him, they took from me the use of mine own house; charged me, on pain of perpetual displeasure, neither to speak of him, entreat for him, nor any way sustain him.

Edm. Most savage, and unnatural!   7

Glo. Go to! say you nothing. There is division between the dukes, and a worse matter than that. I have received a letter this night. 'Tis dangerous to be spoken; I have locked the letter in my closet. These injuries the king now bears will be revenged home; there's part of a power already footed. We must incline to the king. I will look him and privily relieve him. Go you and maintain talk with the duke, that my charity be not of him perceived. If he ask for me, I am ill and gone to bed. If I die for it (as no less is threatened me), the king, my old master, must be relieved. There is strange things toward, Edmund. Pray you, be careful.   20

Exit.

Edm. This courtesy, forbid thee, shall the duke

---

12 home: *to the hilt*
13 power: *army*   footed: *on foot, landed*
14 look: *look for*

Instantly know; and of that letter too.
This seems a fair deserving, and must draw me
That which my father loses: no less than all.   24
The younger rises when the old doth fall.   *Exit.*

SCENE FOURTH

[The Heath. Before a Hovel]

Enter Lear, Kent, and Fool.

Kent. Here is the place, my lord; good my lord, enter.
The tyranny of the open night's too rough
For nature to endure.   *Storm still.*
    Lear.   Let me alone.
    Kent. Good my lord, enter here.
    Lear.   Wilt break my heart?   4
    Kent. I'd rather break mine own. Good my lord, enter.
    Lear. Thou think'st 'tis much that this contentious storm
Invades us to the skin. So 'tis to thee;
But where the greater malady is fix'd,   8
The lesser is scarce felt. Thou'dst shun a bear;
But if thy flight lay toward the roaring sea,
Thou'dst meet the bear i' th' mouth. When the mind's
    free,
The body's delicate. The tempest in my mind   12
Doth from my senses take all feeling else
Save what beats there. Filial ingratitude!
Is it not as this mouth should tear this hand

12 delicate: *fastidious*   15 as: *as if*

For lifting food to't? But I will punish home!   16
No, I will weep no more. ⟨In such a night
To shut me out! Pour on! I will endure.⟩
In such a night as this! O Regan, Goneril!
Your old kind father, whose frank heart gave you all,—   20
O, that way madness lies; let me shun that!
No more of that!

   Kent.   Good my lord, enter here.

   Lear. Prithee, go in thyself; seek thine own ease.
This tempest will not give me leave to ponder   24
On things would hurt me more. But I'll go in.
⟨[*To the Fool.*] In, boy; go first.   *Exit* [*Fool*].
                      You houseless poverty,—
[*To Kent.*] Nay, get thee in. I'll pray, and then I'll sleep.⟩
Poor naked wretches, wheresoe'er you are,   28
That bide the pelting of this pitiless storm,
How shall your houseless heads and unfed sides,
Your loop'd and window'd raggedness, defend you   31
From seasons such as these? O! I have ta'en
Too little care of this. Take physic, pomp;
Expose thyself to feel what wretches feel,
That thou mayst shake the superflux to them,
And show the heavens more just.

   ⟨*Edg.* [*within*]. Fathom and half, fathom and half!
     Poor Tom!⟩

   Fool [*within*]. Come not in here, nuncle. Here's a
     spirit.
Help me! help me!   39

   Kent. Give me thy hand. Who's there?

17–19 *Cf. n.*   19 *Cf. n.*
31 loop'd: *full of holes*
35 shake the superflux: *scatter your superfluities; cf. n.*

Fool [*within*]. A spirit, a spirit! He says his name's poor
    Tom.

Kent. What art thou that dost grumble there i' th'
    straw?
Come forth.   43

Enter Edgar and Fool.

Edg. Away! the foul fiend follows me! Through
the sharp hawthorn blows the cold wind. Hum! go
to thy bed and warm thee.

Lear. Didst thou give all to thy daughters? And
art thou come to this?   48

Edg. Who gives anything to poor Tom, whom the
foul fiend hath led through fire and ⟨through flame,⟩
through ford and whirlpool, o'er bog and quagmire?
that hath laid knives under his pillow, and halters in
his pew; set ratsbane by his porridge; made him
proud of heart, to ride on a bay trotting-horse over
four-inched bridges, to course his own shadow for a
traitor. Bless thy five wits! Tom's a-cold. ⟨O! do de,
do de, do de.⟩ Bless thee from whirlwinds, star-
blasting, and taking! Do poor Tom some charity,
whom the foul fiend vexes. There could I have him
now, and there, and there again, and there.

                                              Storm still.
Lear. What! has his daughters brought him to this pass?
Could'st thou save nothing? Would'st thou give 'em all?

Fool. Nay, he reserved a blanket. Else we had
been all shamed.   64

---

52 halters in his pew; *cf. n.*   55 course: *hunt*
58 taking: *influence of malignant powers*
59 There . . . now; *cf. n.*

Lear. Now all the plagues that in the pendulous air
Hang fated o'er men's faults light on thy daughters!

Kent. He hath no daughters, sir.   67

Lear. Death, traitor! nothing could have súbdu'd nature
To such a lowness, but his unkind daughters.
Is it the fashion that discarded fathers
Should have thus little mercy on their flesh?   71
Judicious punishment! 'twas this flesh begot
Those pelican daughters.

Edg. Pillicock sat on Pillicock-hill:
Halloo, halloo, loo, loo!   75

Fool. This cold night will turn us all to fools and madmen.

Edg. Take heed o' th' foul fiend. Obey thy parents; keep thy word justly; swear not; commit not with man's sworn spouse; set not thy sweet heart on proud array. Tom's a-cold.   81

Lear. What hast thou been?

Edg. A servingman, proud in heart and mind, that curled my hair, wore gloves in my cap, served the lust of my mistress's heart, and did the act of darkness with her; swore as many oaths as I spake words, and broke them in the sweet face of heaven; one that slept in the contriving of lust, and waked to do it. Wine loved I deeply, dice dearly, and in woman out-paramoured the Turk: false of heart, light of ear, bloody of hand; hog in sloth, fox in stealth, wolf in greediness, dog in madness, lion in prey. Let not the creaking of shoes nor the rustling of silks betray thy

65 pendulous: *overhanging*   66 fated: *by fate's will*
73 pelican; *cf. n.*   74 Pillicock; *cf. n.*

poor heart to woman. Keep thy foot out of brothels,
thy hand out of plackets, thy pen from lenders' books,
and defy the foul fiend. Still through the hawthorn
blows the cold wind! Hay no nonny, Dolphin my
boy! my boy, sessa! let him trot by.   *Storm still.*

Lear. Why, thou wert better in thy grave than to
answer with thy uncovered body this extremity of the
skies. Is man no more than this? Consider him well.
Thou owest the worm no silk, the beast no hide, the
sheep no wool, the cat no perfume. Ha! here's three
on's are sophisticated; thou art the thing itself. Unaccommodated man is no more but such a poor, bare,
forked animal as thou art. Off, off, you lendings!
Come; unbutton here.   107

[*Tearing off his clothes.*]

Fool. Prithee, nuncle, be contented. 'Tis a naughty
night to swim in. Now a little fire in a wild field were
like an old lecher's heart; a small spark, all the rest
on's body cold. Look! here comes a walking fire.   111

Enter Gloucester with a torch.

Edg. This is the foul fiend Flibbertigibbet. He begins at curfew, and walks till the first cock. He gives
the web and the pin, squints the eye, and makes the
harelip; mildews the white wheat, and hurts the
poor creature of earth.   116

97, 98 Hay . . . sessa; *cf. n.*
103 cat: *civet-cat*
104 Unaccommodated: *unequipped*
109 wild: *blustery* (cf. II.iv.309)
112 Flibbertigibbet: *one of Harsnet's devils*
114 web and the pin: *eye-disease*

Swithold footed thrice the old;
He met the night-mare, and her nine-fold;
Bid her alight,
And her troth plight,
And aroint thee, witch, aroint thee!

Kent. How fares your Grace?   122

Lear. What's he?

Kent. Who's there? What is't you seek?

Glo. What are you there? Your names?

Edg. Poor Tom, that eats the swimming frog, the toad, the tadpole, the wall-newt, and the water; that in the fury of his heart, when the foul fiend rages, eats cow-dung for sallets, swallows the old rat and the ditch-dog; drinks the green mantle of the standing pool; who is whipped from tithing to tithing, and stock-punished, and imprisoned; who hath had three suits to his back, six shirts to his body,   133

Horse to ride, and weapon to wear.
But mice and rats and such small deer
Have been Tom's food for seven long year.

Beware my follower. Peace, Smulkin! peace, thou fiend.   138

Glo. What! hath your Grace no better company?

Edg. The prince of darkness is a gentleman;
Modo he's call'd, and Mahu.

117 Swithold: *St. Withold, St. Vitalis*   old: *wold, moor-land*
118 nine-fold: *nine followers*
120 her troth plight: *pledge her troth*
121 aroint: *get out!*
127 wall-newt: *lizard*   water: *water-newt*
129 sallets: *salads*
130 ditch-dog: *dead dog in a ditch*   standing: *stagnant*
131 tithing: *district*
135 deer: *game*   137 Smulkin; *cf. n.*

Glo. Our flesh and blood, my lord, is grown so vile,
That it doth hate what gets it.   143
    Edg. Poor Tom's a-cold.
    Glo. Go in with me. My duty cannot suffer
T'obey in all your daughters' hard commands.
Though their injunction be to bar my doors,   147
And let this tyrannous night take hold upon you,
Yet have I ventur'd to come seek you out
And bring you where both fire and food is ready.
    Lear. First let me talk with this philosopher.   151
What is the cause of thunder?
    Kent.   Good my lord,
Take his offer. Go into the house.
    Lear. I'll talk a word with this most learned Theban.
What is your study?   155
    Edg. How to prevent the fiend, and to kill vermin.
    Lear. Let me ask you one word in private.
    Kent. Impórtune him once more to go, my lord.
His wits begin t'unsettle.
    Glo.   Canst thou blame him? *Storm still.*
His daughters seek his death. Ah, that good Kent!   160
He said it would be thus, poor banish'd man.
Thou say'st the king grows mad. I'll tell thee, friend:
I am almost mad myself. I had a son,   163
Now outlaw'd from my blood—he sought my life
But lately, very late. I lov'd him, friend;
No father his son dearer. True to tell thee,
The grief hath craz'd my wits. What a night's this!   167
I do beseech your Grace,—

146 in all: *in every respect*
163–167 Cf. *n.*
168 cry you mercy: *I beg your pardon*

Lear.   O, cry you mercy, sir.
Noble philosopher, your company.

Edg. Tom's a-cold.

Glo. In, fellow, there, into th' hovel. Keep thee warm.

Lear. Come, let's in all.

Kent.   This way, my lord.

Lear.   With him!
I will keep still with my philosopher.   173

Kent. Good my lord, soothe him. Let him take the fellow.

Glo. Take him you on.

Kent. Sirrah, come on; go along with us.   176

Lear. Come, good Athenian.

Glo.   No words, no words. Hush.

Edg.   Child Rowland to the dark tower came,
           His word was still, Fie, foh, and fum,
           I smell the blood of a British man.   180

                                        Exeunt.

SCENE FIFTH

[Gloucester's Castle]

Enter Cornwall and Edmund.

Corn. I will have my revenge ere I depart the
house.

Edm. How, my lord, I may be censured, that
nature thus gives way to loyalty, something fears me
to think of.   5

Corn. I now perceive it was not altogether your

178–180 Cf. n.   180 British man; cf. n.
3 censured: *judged*   4 something fears me: *I somewhat fear*

brother's evil disposition made him seek his death;
but a provoking merit, set a-work by a reprovable
badness in himself.   9

Edm. How malicious is my fortune that I must re-
pent to be just! This is the letter he spoke of, which
approves him an intelligent party to the advantages
of France. O heavens! that this treason were not, or
not I the detector!   14

Corn. Go with me to the duchess.

Edm. If the matter of this paper be certain, you
have mighty business in hand.   17

Corn. True or false, it hath made thee Earl of
Gloucester. Seek out where thy father is, that he
may be ready for our apprehension.   20

Edm. [*aside*]. If I find him comforting the king,
it will stuff his suspicion more fully.—I will per-
sever in my course of loyalty, though the conflict be
sore between that and my blood.   24

Corn. I will lay trust upon thee, and thou shalt
find a dearer father in my love.   *Exeunt.*

SCENE SIXTH

[*A Farmhouse near Gloucester's Castle*]

Enter Kent and Gloucester.

Glo. Here is better than the open air; take it thank-
fully. I will piece out the comfort with what addition
I can. I will not be long from you.   3

---

 provoking merit: *meritorious incitement*
.2 intelligent party: *conscious accessory*

Kent. All the power of his wits have given way to his impatience. The gods reward your kindness!

Exit [Gloucester].

Enter Lear, Edgar, and Fool.

Edg. Fraretto calls me, and tells me Nero is an angler in the lake of darkness. Pray, innocent, and beware the foul fiend.   8

Fool. Prithee, nuncle, tell me whether a madman be a gentleman or a yeoman.

Lear. A king, a king!

⟨*Fool.* No, he's a yeoman that has a gentleman to his son; for he's a mad yeoman that sees his son a gentleman before him.

Lear.⟩ To have a thousand with red burning spits
Come hizzing in upon 'em,—   16

«*Edg.* The foul fiend bites my back.

Fool. He's mad that trusts in the tameness of a wolf, a horse's health, a boy's love, or a whore's oath.

Lear. It shall be done! I will arraign them straight.   20
[*To Edgar.*] Come, sit thou here, most learned justicer.
⟨*To the Fool.*] Thou, sapient sir, sit here. No, you she foxes!

Edg. Look, where he stands and glares! Want'st thou eyes? At trial, madam!   24

Come o'er the broom, Bessy, to me,—

Fool.   Her boat hath a leak,
                And she must not speak
        Why she dares not come over to thee.

4 have; *cf. n.*
5 impatience: *inability to endure*
5 S.d. *Cf. n.*   6 Fraretto; *cf. n.*
7 innocent: *the Fool*   16 hizzing: *whizzing*

Edg. The foul fiend haunts poor Tom in the voice
of a nightingale. Hoppedance cries in Tom's belly for
two white herring. Croak not, black angel. I have no
food for thee.   32

Kent. How do you, sir? Stand you not so amaz'd.
Will you lie down and rest upon the cushions?

Lear. I'll see their trial first. Bring in their evidence.
[*To Edgar.*] Thou robed man of justice, take thy place; 36
[*To the Fool.*] And thou, his yoke-fellow of equity,
Bench by his side. [*To Kent.*] You are o' th' commission.
Sit you too.

Edg. Let us deal justly.   40

> Sleepest or wakest thou, jolly shepherd?
>   Thy sheep be in the corn;
> And for one blast of thy minikin mouth,
>   Thy sheep shall take no harm.

Purr! the cat is grey.   45

Lear. Arraign her first. 'Tis Goneril, I here take
my oath before this honorable assembly, kicked the
poor king her father.   48

Fool. Come hither, mistress. Is your name Goneril?

Lear. She cannot deny it.

Fool. Cry you mercy, I took you for a joint-stool.

Lear. And here's another, whose warp'd looks proclaim
What store her heart is made on. Stop her there!   53
Arms! arms! sword! fire! Corruption in the place!
False justicer, why hast thou let her 'scape?»

---

25 broom; *cf. n.*   33 amaz'd: *confused*
38 o' th' commission: *one of the delegated judges*
41–44 Cf. *n.*
43 minikin: *mignonne, pretty*   45 Cf. *n.*
46–48 Cf. *n.*   51 joint-stool; *cf. n.*

Edg. Bless thy five wits!   56

Kent. O pity! Sir, where is the patience now
That you so oft have boasted to retain?

Edg. [*aside*]. My tears begin to take his part so much,
They'll mar my counterfeiting.   60

Lear. The little dogs and all,
Trey, Blanch, and Sweet-heart, see, they bark at me.

Edg. Tom will throw his head at them. Avaunt,
you curs!   64

> Be thy mouth or black or white,
> Tooth that poisons if it bite;
> Mastiff, greyhound, mongrel grim,
> Hound or spaniel, brach or him,
> Or bobtail tike or trundle-tail;
> Tom will make them weep and wail:
> For, with throwing thus my head,
> Dogs leap the hatch, and all are fled.

Do de, de, de. Sessa! Come, march to wakes and
fairs and market-towns. Poor Tom, thy horn is dry.   74

Lear. Then let them anatomize Regan. See what
breeds about her heart. Is there any cause in nature
that makes these hard hearts? [*To Edgar.*] You, sir, I
entertain for one of my hundred; only I do not like
the fashion of your garments. You will say, they are
Persian, but let them be changed.   80

Kent. Now, good my lord, lie here and rest awhile.

Lear. Make no noise, make no noise. Draw the cur-

---

65 or . . . or: *either . . . or*
68 brach or him: *female dog or he-dog; cf. n.*
69 bobtail tike: *short-tail cur*   trundle-tail: *curly-tail*
72 hatch: *lower half of the house-door*
73 wakes: *church festivals*
78 entertain: *employ*   hundred: *i.e., knights*
80 Persian; *cf. n.*

tains: so! so! We'll go to supper i' th' morning. «So!
so! so!»   84

(*Fool.* And I'll go to bed at noon.)

Enter Gloucester.

Glo. Come hither, friend. Where is the king my
master?

Kent. Here, sir; but trouble him not, his wits are
gone.   89

Glo. Good friend, I prithee, take him in thy arms.
I have o'erheard a plot of death upon him.
There is a litter ready; lay him in't,
And drive toward Dover, friend, where thou shalt meet
Both welcome and protection. Take up thy master: 94
If thou shouldst dally half an hour, his life,
With thine and all that offer to defend him,
Stand in assured loss. Take up, take up;   97
And follow me, that will to some provision
Give thee quick conduct.

«*Kent.*   Oppress'd nature sleeps.
This rest might yet have balm'd thy broken sinews,
Which, if convenience will not allow,   101
Stand in hard cure.—[*To the Fool.*] Come, help to bear
       thy master;
Thou must not stay behind.

Glo.»   Come, come, away.

Exeunt [all but Edgar].

«*Edg.* When we our betters see bearing our woes,
We scarcely think our miseries our foes.   105

83 *Cf. n.*   85 *Cf. n.*   97 in assured loss: *sure to be lost*
99 conduct: *guidance*
100 sinews: *nerves*   102 in hard cure: *hard to cure*

Who alone suffers suffers most i' th' mind,
Leaving free things and happy shows behind;
But then the mind much sufferance doth o'erskip,
When grief hath mates, and bearing fellowship.   109
How light and portable my pain seems now,
When that which makes me bend makes the king bow,
He childed as I father'd! Tom, away!
Mark the high noises, and thyself bewray   113
When false opinion, whose wrong thought defiles thee,
In thy just proof repeals and reconciles thee.
What will hap more to-night, safe 'scape the king!
Lurk, lurk!»   [Exit.]

SCENE SEVENTH

[Gloucester's Castle]

Enter Cornwall, Regan, Goneril, Bastard [Edmund],
                    and Servants.

   Corn. Post speedily to my lord your husband. Show
him this letter. The army of France is landed. Seek
out the traitor Gloucester.

                    [Exeunt some of the Servants.]

   Reg. Hang him instantly.   4
   Gon. Pluck out his eyes.
   Corn. Leave him to my displeasure. Edmund, keep
you our sister company: the revenges we are bound

---

109 bearing: *suffering*   110 portable: *endurable*
113 high noises: *great tumults*   115 repeals: *recalls*
116 What . . . more: *whatever else*
117 Lurk, lurk; *cf. n.*

to take upon your traitorous father are not fit for
your beholding. Advise the duke, where you are
going, to a most festinate preparation. We are bound
to the like. Our posts shall be swift and intelligent
betwixt us. Farewell, dear sister; farewell, my Lord
of Gloucester.   13

Enter Steward [Oswald].

How now? Where's the king?
  Osw. My Lord of Gloucester hath convey'd him hence.
Some five or six and thirty of his knights,   16
Hot questrists after him, met him at gate;
Who, with some other of the lord's dependants,
Are gone with him toward Dover, where they boast
To have well-armed friends.
  Corn.   Get horses for your mistress.   20
  Gon. Farewell, sweet lord, and sister.
  Corn. Edmund, farewell.
              Ex. Goneril, Edmund [and Oswald].
               Go seek the traitor Gloucester,
Pinion him like a thief, bring him before us.
              [Exeunt other Servants.]
Though well we may not pass upon his life   24
Without the form of justice, yet our power
Shall do a courtesy to our wrath, which men
May blame but not control.

Enter Gloucester, brought in by two or three.

              Who's there? The traitor?
  Reg. Ingrateful fox! 'tis he.

10 festinate: *speedy*
17 questrists: *searchers*

Corn.   Bind fast his corky arms. 28

Glo. What means your Graces? Good my friends, consider

You are my guests. Do me no foul play, friends.

Corn. Bind him, I say.   [*Servants bind him.*]

Reg.   Hard, hard. O filthy traitor!

Glo. Unmerciful lady as you are, I'm none. 32

Corn. To this chair bind him. Villain, thou shalt find—

            [*Regan plucks his beard.*]

Glo. By the kind gods, 'tis most ignobly done

To pluck me by the beard.

Reg. So white, and such a traitor!

Glo.   Naughty lady, 36

These hairs which thou dost ravish from my chin

Will quicken and accuse thee. I am your host.

With robbers' hands my hospitable favors

You should not ruffle thus. What will you do? 40

Corn. Come, sir, what letters had you late from France?

Reg. Be simple-answer'd, for we know the truth.

Corn. And what confederacy have you with the traitors

Late footed in the kingdom? 44

Reg. To whose hands have you sent the lunatic king?

Speak.

Glo. I have a letter guessingly set down,

Which came from one that's of a neutral heart, 48

And not from one oppos'd.

Corn.   Cunning.

Reg.   And false.

---

28 corky: *dry, withered*   36 Naughty: *wicked*
38 quicken: *come to life*   39 favors: *features*
42 simple-answer'd; *cf. n.*
47 guessingly: *expressed in conjectural language*

Corn. Where hast thou sent the king?

Glo.   To Dover.

Reg. Wherefore to Dover? Wast thou not charg'd at
    peril—

Corn. Wherefore to Dover? Let him answer that.   52

Glo. I am tied to th' stake, and I must stand the course.

Reg. Wherefore to Dover?

Glo. Because I would not see thy cruel nails

Pluck out his poor old eyes, nor thy fierce sister   56

In his anointed flesh rash boarish fangs.

The sea, with such a storm as his bow'd head

In hell-black night endur'd, would have buoy'd up,

And quench'd the stelled fires;   60

Yet, poor old heart, he holp the heavens to rage.

If wolves had at thy gate howl'd that dern time,

Thou shouldst have said, 'Good porter, turn the key.'

All cruels else subscribe, but I shall see   64

The winged vengeance overtake such children.

Corn. See't shalt thou never. Fellows, hold the chair,

Upon those eyes of thine I'll set my foot.

Glo. He that will think to live till he be old,   68

Give me some help! O cruel! O you gods!

                               [*Gloucester's eye put out.*]

Reg. One side will mock another. Th' other too.

Corn. If you see vengeance—

Servant.   Hold your hand, my lord!

I have serv'd you ever since I was a child,   72

---

53 course: *an attack in the sport of bear-baiting*
57 rash: *push violently, slash; cf.* n.
58 bow'd; *cf.* n.   59 buoy'd: *surged*
60 stelled fires: *fixed stars; cf.* n.
62 dern: *dreary*
64 subscribe: *sanction; cf.* n.   71 Hold your hand; *cf.* n.

But better service have I never done you
Than now to bid you hold.

  Reg.   How now, you dog?

  Serv. If you did wear a beard upon your chin,
I'd shake it on this quarrel. What do you mean— 76

  Corn. My villain!

  Serv. Nay then, come on, and take the chance of anger.
      Draw and fight. [*Cornwall is wounded.*]

  Reg. Give me thy sword. A peasant stand up thus!
     She takes a sword and runs at him behind.

  Serv. O, I am slain! My lord, you have one eye left 80
To see some mischief on him. O!

  Corn. Lest it see more, prevent it. Out, vile jelly!
Where is thy lustre now?

  Glo. All dark and comfortless. Where's my son Ed-
  mund?   84
Edmund, enkindle all the sparks of nature
To quit this horrid act.

  Reg.   Out, treacherous villain!
Thou call'st on him that hates thee. It was he
That made the overture of thy treasons to us, 88
Who is too good to pity thee.

  Glo. O my follies! Then Edgar was abus'd.
Kind gods, forgive me that, and prosper him!

  Reg. Go thrust him out at gates, and let him smell 92
His way to Dover. *Exit* [*Attendant*] *with Gloucester.*
How is't, my lord? How look you?

  Corn. I have receiv'd a hurt. Follow me, lady.
Turn out that eyeless villain. Throw this slave
Upon the dunghill. Regan, I bleed apace: 96

86 quit: *requite*
88 overture: *exposure*

Untimely comes this hurt. Give me your arm.

                     Exeunt [Cornwall and Regan].

«*2nd Serv.* I'll never care what wickedness I do
If this man come to good.

    3rd Serv.   If she live long,
And, in the end, meet the old course of death,   100
Women will all turn monsters.

    2nd Serv. Let's follow the old earl, and get the bedlam
To lead him where he would. His roguish madness
Allows itself to anything.   104

    3rd Serv. Go thou. I'll fetch some flax and whites of
      eggs
To apply to his bleeding face. Now, heaven help him!

                             Exeunt.»

ACT FOURTH

SCENE FIRST

[The Heath]

Enter Edgar.

  Edg. Yet better thus, and known to be contemn'd,
Than still contemn'd and flatter'd. To be worst,
The lowest and most dejected thing of fortune,
Stands still in esperance, lives not in fear.   4

100 old: *familiar, regular*
102 bedlam: *bedlam-beggar (Edgar)*
103 would: *would be led*
1 known . . . contemn'd: *openly despised*
4 esperance: *hope*

The lamentable change is from the best;
The worst returns to laughter. ⟨Welcome, then,
Thou unsubstantial air that I embrace.
The wretch that thou hast blown unto the worst   8
Owes nothing to thy blasts.⟩ But who comes here?

Enter Gloucester, led by an old man.

My father, poorly led? World, world, O world!
But that thy strange mutations make us hate thee,
Life would not yield to age.

    Old Man.   O my good lord!   12
I have been your tenant, and your father's tenant,
These fourscore years.

    Glo. Away! Get thee away! Good friend, be gone.
Thy comforts can do me no good at all;   16
Thee they may hurt.

    Old Man.   You cannot see your way.

    Glo. I have no way, and therefore want no eyes.
I stumbled when I saw. Full oft 'tis seen,
Our means secure us, and our mere defects   20
Prove our commodities. O dear son Edgar,
The food of thy abused father's wrath!
Might I but live to see thee in my touch,
I'd say I had eyes again.

    Old Man.   How now! Who's there?   24

    Edg. [*aside*]. O gods! Who is't can say, 'I am at the
    worst?'

I am worse than e'er I was.

6 The . . . laughter; *cf. n.*
9 Owes nothing: *has nothing more to pay*
10 poorly led; *cf. n.*   11, 12 But that . . . age; *cf. n.*
20, 21 means . . . commodities; *cf. n.*

Old Man.   'Tis poor mad Tom.

Edg. [*aside*]. And worse I may be yet. The worst is not,
So long as we can say, 'This is the worst.'   28

Old Man. Fellow, where goest?

Glo.   Is it a beggar-man?

Old Man. Madman and beggar too.

Glo. He has some reason, else he could not beg.
I' th' last night's storm I such a fellow saw,   32
Which made me think a man a worm. My son
Came then into my mind; and yet my mind
Was then scarce friends with him. I have heard more
    since.
As flies to wanton boys, are we to th' gods: 36
They kill us for their sport.

Edg. [*aside*].   How should this be?
Bad is the trade that must play fool to sorrow,
Angering itself and others.—[*To Gloucester.*] Bless thee,
    master!

Glo. Is that the naked fellow?

Old Man.   Ay, my lord.

Glo. Then, prithee, get thee gone. If, for my sake,   41
Thou wilt o'ertake us, hence a mile or twain,
I' th' way toward Dover, do it for ancient love;
And bring some covering for this naked soul   44
Which I'll entreat to lead me.

Old Man.   Alack, sir! he is mad.

Glo. 'Tis the times' plague, when madmen lead the
    blind.
Do as I bid thee, or rather do thy pleasure;
Above the rest, be gone.   48

45 Which: *whom* ('who' Q)

Old Man. I'll bring him the best 'parel that I have,
Come on't what will.   *Exit.*

Glo. Sirrah, naked fellow,—

Edg. Poor Tom's a-cold. [*Aside.*] I cannot daub it further.   52

Glo. Come hither, fellow.

Edg. ⟨And yet I must.⟩ Bless thy sweet eyes, they bleed.

Glo. Know'st thou the way to Dover?   55

  Edg. Both stile and gate, horse-way and footpath.
Poor Tom hath been scared out of his good wits. Bless
thee, good man's son, from the foul fiend! «Five
fiends have been in poor Tom at once: of lust, as
Obidicut; Hobbididance, prince of dumbness; Mahu,
of stealing; Modo, of murder; Flibbertigibbet, of mopping and mowing, who since possesses chambermaids
and waiting-women. So, bless thee, master!»

Glo. Here, take this purse, thou whom the heavens'
  plagues   64
Have humbled to all strokes. That I am wretched
Makes thee the happier. Heavens, deal so still!
Let the superfluous and lust-dieted man,
That slaves your ordinance, that will not see   68
Because he does not feel, feel your power quickly.
So distribution should undo excess,
And each man have enough. Dost thou know Dover?

  Edg. Ay, master.   72

Glo. There is a cliff, whose high and bending head
Looks fearfully in the confined deep.

51 daub it: *make poor pretence*
61, 62 mopping and mowing: *making grimaces*
67–71 Cf. *n.*
67 superfluous and lust-dieted: *over-rich and wilful*
68 slaves; *cf. n.*   74 in the confined deep; *cf. n.*

Bring me but to the very brim of it,
And I'll repair the misery thou dost bear   76
With something rich about me. From that place
I shall no leading need.
    Edg.   Give me thy arm.
Poor Tom shall lead thee.   *Exeunt.*

SCENE SECOND

[Before Albany's Palace]

Enter Goneril and Bastard [Edmund].

    Gon. Welcome, my lord! I marvel our mild husband
Not met us on the way.   *Enter Steward [Oswald].*
                Now, where's your master?
    Osw. Madam, within; but never man so chang'd.
I told him of the army that was landed;   4
He smil'd at it. I told him you were coming;
His answer was, 'The worse!' Of Gloucester's treachery,
And of the loyal service of his son,
When I inform'd him, then he call'd me sot,   8
And told me I had turn'd the wrong side out.
What most he should dislike seems pleasant to him;
What like, offensive.
    Gon. [*to Edmund*]. Then shall you go no further.
It is the cowish terror of his spirit   12
That dares not undertake. He'll not feel wrongs

1 Welcome; *cf. n.*   3 never man so chang'd; *cf. n.*
9 turn'd . . . out: *inverted right and wrong*
12 cowish: *easily cowed*   13 undertake: *assert itself*

Which tie him to an answer. Our wishes on the way
May prove effects. Back, Edmund, to my brother;
Hasten his musters and conduct his powers.   16
I must change names at home, and give the distaff
Into my husband's hands. This trusty servant
Shall pass between us. Ere long you are like to hear
(If you dare venture in your own behalf)   20
A mistress's command. Wear this.   [*Giving a jewel.*]
                              Spare speech;
Decline your head. This kiss, if it durst speak,
Would stretch thy spirits up into the air.
Conceive, and fare thee well.   24

   Edm. Yours in the ranks of death.

   Gon.   My most dear Gloucester!
                              Exit [*Edmund*].

〈O the difference of man and man!〉
To thee a woman's services are due;
My foot usurps my body.

   Osw.   Madam, here comes my lord.
                              Exit Steward.

                    Enter Albany.

   Gon. I have been worth the whistling.

   Alb.   O, Goneril,   29
You are not worth the dust which the rude wind
Blows in your face. «I fear your disposition.

14 tie him to: *require*
15 brother: *brother-in-law* (Cornwall)
17 names: *i.e., of husband and wife; cf. n.*
21 mistress's; *cf. n.*   Spare speech: *say nothing*
22 Decline: *bend down*
24 Conceive: *interpret my meaning*
28 My . . . body; *cf. n.*   29 worth the whistling; *cf. n.*
31 fear: *fear for*

That nature, which contemns it origin,   32
Cannot be border'd certain in itself;
She that herself will sliver and disbranch
From her material sap, perforce must wither
And come to deadly use.   36
   Gon. No more; the text is foolish.
   Alb. Wisdom and goodness to the vile seem vile;
Filths savor but themselves. What have you done?
Tigers, not daughters, what have you perform'd?   40
A father, and a gracious aged man,
Whose reverence even the head-lugg'd bear would lick,
Most barbarous, most degenerate! have you madded.
Could my good brother suffer you to do it?   44
A man, a prince, by him so benefited!
If that the heavens do not their visible spirits
Send quickly down to tame these vile offences,
It will come,   48
Humanity must perforce prey on itself,
Like monsters of the deep.»
   Gon.   Milk-liver'd man!
That bear'st a cheek for blows, a head for wrongs;
Who hast not in thy brows an eye discerning   52
Thine honor from thy suffering! «that not know'st
Fools do those villains pity who are punish'd
Ere they have done their mischief. Where's thy drum?

---

32 it: *its; cf. n.*
33 border'd certain: *possessed of fixed limits or standards of con-*
    duct   34 sliver and disbranch: *split and sever*
35 material: *that of which she is made*
36 come . . . use: *grow poisonous*   39 *Cf. n.*
42 head-lugg'd: *led about by a muzzle*
45 A man: *i.e., Cornwall*   him: *i.e., Lear*
51 *Cf. n.*   52, 53 discerning . . . suffering; *cf. n.*
54, 55 Fools . . . mischief; *cf. n.*

France spreads his banners in our noiseless land,   56
With plumed helm thy state begins to threat,
Whilst thou, a moral fool, sits still, and cries
'Alack! why does he so?'»

Alb.   See thyself, devil!
Proper deformity shows not in the fiend   60
So horrid as in woman.

    Gon.   O vain fool!

    «*Alb.* Thou changed and self-cover'd thing, for shame,
Be-monster not thy feature. Were't my fitness
To let these hands obey my blood,   64
They are apt enough to dislocate and tear
Thy flesh and bones. Howe'er thou art a fiend,
A woman's shape doth shield thee.

    Gon. Marry! Your manhood!—Mew!»   68

Enter a Messenger.

    «*Alb.* What news?»

    Mess. O my good lord, the Duke of Cornwall's dead;
Slain by his servant, going to put out
The other eye of Gloucester.

    Alb.   Gloucester's eyes!   72

    Mess. A servant that he bred, thrill'd with remorse,
Oppos'd against the act, bending his sword
To his great master; who, thereat enrag'd,

56 noiseless: *peaceful, unready*
57 state . . . threat; *cf. n.*   58 moral: *moralizing*
60 Proper deformity: *inherent ugliness*
61 vain: *empty*   62 self-cover'd: *hypocritical*
63 Be-monster not thy feature: *don't let your whole appearance
    become beastly*   my fitness: *what is seemly in me*
64 blood: *passion*   65 apt: *ready*
66 Howe'er: *notwithstanding that*
68 Mew; *cf. n.*   73 remorse: *pity*

Flew on him, and amongst them fell'd him dead,   76
But not without that harmful stroke which since
Hath pluck'd him after.
   Alb.   This shows you are above,
You justicers, that these our nether crimes
So speedily can venge! But, O poor Gloucester!   80
Lost he his other eye?
   Mess.   Both, both, my lord.
This letter, madam, craves a speedy answer.
'Tis from your sister.
   Gon. [*aside*].   One way I like this well;
But being widow, and my Gloucester with her,   84
May all the building in my fancy pluck
Upon my hateful life. Another way
This news is not so tart. [*To Messenger.*] I'll read and
    answer.   *Exit.*
   Alb. Where was his son when they did take his eyes?
   Mess. Come with my lady hither.
   Alb.   He is not here.   89
   Mess. No, my good lord; I met him back again.
   Alb. Knows he the wickedness?
   Mess. Ay, my good lord. 'Twas he inform'd against
    him,   92
And quit the house on purpose that their punishment
Might have the freer course.
   Alb.   Gloucester, I live
To thank thee for the love thou show'dst the king
And to revenge thine eyes. Come hither, friend.
Tell me what more thou know'st.   *Exeunt.*

90 back: *on the way back*

«[SCENE THIRD

Near Dover]

Enter Kent and a Gentleman.

Kent. Why the King of France is so suddenly gone
back know you no reason?

Gent. Something he left imperfect in the state,
which since his coming forth is thought of; which
imports to the kingdom so much fear and danger
that his personal return was most required and necessary.   7

Kent. Who hath he left behind him general?

Gent. The Marshal of France, Monsieur la Far.

Kent. Did your letters pierce the queen to any
demonstration of grief?   11

Gent. Ay, sir; she took them, read them in my presence;
And now and then an ample tear trill'd down
Her delicate cheek. It seem'd she was a queen
Over her passion, who most rebel-like
Sought to be king o'er her.

Kent.   O, then it mov'd her?   16

Gent. Not to a rage. Patience and sorrow strove
Who should express her goodliest. You have seen
Sunshine and rain at once; her smiles and tears
Were like a better way. Those happy smilets   20
That play'd on her ripe lip seem'd not to know

Scene Third; *cf. n.*   12 Ay, sir; *cf. n.*
15 who: *which*
20 better way: *like sunshine and rain, but in a nobler way*

What guests were in her eyes, which parted thence
As pearls from diamonds dropp'd. In brief,
Sorrow would be a rarity most belov'd,   24
If all could so become it.

 Kent.   Made she no verbal question?

 Gent. Faith, once or twice she heav'd the name of
  'father'
Pantingly forth, as if it press'd her heart;
Cried, 'Sisters! sisters! Shame of ladies! sisters!   28
Kent! father! sisters! What, i' th' storm? i' th' night?
Let pity not believe't!' There she shook
The holy water from her heavenly eyes
And clamor-moisten'd hair. Then away she started   32
To deal with grief alone.

 Kent.   It is the stars,
The stars above us, govern our conditions.
Else one self mate and make could not beget
Such different issues. You spoke not with her since? 36

 Gent. No.

 Kent. Was this before the king return'd?

 Gent.   No, since.

 Kent. Well, sir, the poor distressed Lear's i' th' town,
Who sometime, in his better tune, remembers   40
What we are come about, and by no means
Will yield to see his daughter.

 Gent.   Why, good sir?

 Kent. A sovereign shame so elbows him: his own unkindness,

22 which: *i.e., the 'guests' (tears)*
25 verbal question: *oral conversation* 30 believe 't; *cf. n.*
32 clamor-moisten'd: *wet with lamentation; cf. n.*
35 mate and make: *husband and wife*
40 sometime . . . tune; *cf. n.* 43 elbows: *jogs, disquiets*

That stripp'd her from his benediction, turn'd her   44
To foreign casualties, gave her dear rights
To his dog-hearted daughters,—these things sting
His mind so venomously that burning shame
Detains him from Cordelia.

    Gent.   Alack, poor gentleman!   48

    Kent. Of Albany's and Cornwall's powers you heard
        not?

    Gent. 'Tis so, they are afoot.

    Kent. Well, sir, I'll bring you to our master Lear,
And leave you to attend him. Some dear cause   52
Will in concealment wrap me up awhile.
When I am known aright, you shall not grieve
Lending me this acquaintance. I pray you, go
Along with me.   *Exeunt.*»

SCENE FOURTH

[A Highroad near Dover]

*Enter with drum and colors, Cordelia, Gentlemen,
Doctor, and Soldiers.*

    Cor. Alack, 'tis he! Why, he was met even now
As mad as the vex'd sea; singing aloud,
Crown'd with rank femiter and furrow weeds,
With hordocks, hemlock, nettles, cuckoo-flowers,
Darnel, and all the idle weeds that grow   4

45 To foreign casualties: *to take chances among foreigners*
50 so, they: *true that they*
3 femiter: *fumitory, plant with bitter taste*
4 hordocks: *burdocks* (?)   cuckoo-flowers: *the ragged robin*
5 Darnel: *a coarse grass*   idle: *worthless*

In our sustaining corn. A century send forth;
Search every acre in the high-grown field,
And bring him to our eye.   [*Exit an Officer.*]
                  What can man's wisdom   8
In the restoring his bereaved sense?
He that helps him take all my outward worth.
    Doct. There is means, madam.
Our foster-nurse of nature is repose,   12
The which he lacks. That to provoke in him
Are many simples operative, whose power
Will close the eye of anguish.
    Cor.   All bless'd secrets,
All you unpublish'd virtues of the earth,   16
Spring with my tears! be aidant and remediate
In the good man's distress! Seek, seek for him,
Lest his ungovern'd rage dissolve the life
That wants the means to lead it.

                 Enter Messenger.

    Mess.   News, madam.   20
The British powers are marching hitherward.
    Cor. 'Tis known before. Our preparation stands
In expectation of them. O dear father,
It is thy business that I go about!   24
Therefore great France
My mourning and important tears hath pitied.
No blown ambition doth our arms incite,
But love, dear love, and our ag'd father's right,
Soon may I hear and see him!   *Exeunt.*

6 century: *company of one hundred men*
14 simples: *medicinal plants*
17 aidant and remediate: *aiding and remedial*
26 important: *importunate*

SCENE FIFTH

[Regan's Palace, Gloucester]

Enter Regan and Steward [Oswald].

Reg. But are my brother's powers set forth?
Osw.   Ay, madam.
Reg. Himself in person there?
Osw.   Madam, with much ado.
Your sister is the better soldier.
Reg. Lord Edmund spake not with your lord at home?
Osw. No, madam.   5
Reg. What might import my sister's letter to him?
Osw. I know not, lady.
Reg. Faith, he is posted hence on serious matter.   8
It was great ignorance, Gloucester's eyes being out,
To let him live. Where he arrives he moves
All hearts against us. Edmund, I think, is gone,
In pity of his misery, to dispatch   12
His nighted life; moreover, to descry
The strength o' th' enemy.
  Osw. I must needs after him, madam, with my letter.
Reg. Our troops set forth to-morrow. Stay with us;   16
The ways are dangerous.
  Osw.   I may not, madam.
My lady charg'd my duty in this business.
Reg. Why should she write to Edmund? Might not you
Transport her purposes by word? Belike,   20

Scene Fifth. S.d. *Cf. n.*
6 import: *be the meaning of*

Some things—I know not what. I'll love thee much,
Let me unseal the letter.

    Osw.   Madam, I had rather—

    Reg. I know your lady does not love her husband.
I am sure of that, and at her late being here   24
She gave strange eliads and most speaking looks
To noble Edmund. I know you are of her bosom.

    Osw. I, madam?

    Reg. I speak in understanding; you are, I know't.   28
Therefore I do advise you, take this note:
My lord is dead; Edmund and I have talk'd,
And more convenient is he for my hand
Than for your lady's. You may gather more.   32
If you do find him, pray you, give him this,
And when your mistress hears thus much from you,
I pray desire her call her wisdom to her.
So, fare you well.   36
If you do chance to hear of that blind traitor,
Preferment falls on him that cuts him off.

    Osw. Would I could meet him, madam! I should show
What party I do follow.

    Reg.   Fare thee well.   *Exeunt.*

---

21 Some things; *cf. n.*   22 I had rather—; *cf. n.*
25 eliads: *œillades, oglings*
26 of her bosom: *in her confidence*
29 take this note: *speak to her in this key*
35 desire . . . her: *i.e., tell her not to be a fool*

SCENE SIXTH

[The Country near Dover]

Enter Gloucester and Edgar.

Glo. When shall I come to th' top of that same hill?
Edg. You do climb up it now. Look how we labor.
Glo. Methinks the ground is even.
Edg.   Horrible steep.
Hark! do you hear the sea?
Glo.   No, truly.   4
Edg. Why, then your other senses grow imperfect
By your eyes' anguish.
Glo.   So may it be, indeed.
Methinks thy voice is alter'd, and thou speak'st
In better phrase and matter than thou didst.   8
Edg. Y'are much deceiv'd. In nothing am I chang'd
But in my garments.
Glo.   Methinks y'are better spoken.
Edg. Come on, sir; here's the place. Stand still.
How fearful   12
And dizzy 'tis to cast one's eyes so low!
The crows and choughs that wing the midway air
Show scarce so gross as beetles. Half way down
Hangs one that gathers samphire, dreadful trade!   16
Methinks he seems no bigger than his head.
The fishermen that walk upon the beach

9 deceiv'd: *mistaken*
14 choughs: *bird of the crow family, jackdaw*
16 samphire: *samper, used for pickles*

Appear like mice, and yond tall anchoring bark
Diminish'd to her cock, her cock a buoy   20
Almost too small for sight. The murmuring surge,
That on th' unnumber'd idle pebble chafes,
Cannot be heard so high. I'll look no more,
Lest my brain turn, and the deficient sight   24
Topple down headlong.

Glo.   Set me where you stand.

Edg. Give me your hand. You are now within a foot
Of th' extreme verge. For all beneath the moon
Would I not leap upright.

Glo.   Let go my hand.   28
Here, friend, 's another purse; in it a jewel
Well worth a poor man's taking. Fairies and gods
Prosper it with thee! Go thou further off.
Bid me farewell, and let me hear thee going.   32

Edg. Now fare ye well, good sir.

Glo.   With all my heart.

Edg. [*aside*]. Why I do trifle thus with his despair
Is done to cure it.

Glo.   O you mighty gods!   *He kneels.*
This world I do renounce, and in your sights   36
Shake patiently my great affliction off.
If I could bear it longer, and not fall
To quarrel with your great opposeless wills,
My snuff and loathed part of nature should   40
Burn itself out. If Edgar live, O, bless him!
Now, fellow, fare thee well.

20 cock: *cock-boat*
22 unnumber'd: *innumerable*   pebble; *cf. n.*
24 deficient sight; *cf. n.*   34, 35 Why . . . cure it; *cf. n.*
39 opposeless: *paramount*   40 snuff; *cf. n.*

Edg.   Gone, sir: farewell.

                                       He [Gloucester] falls.

[*Aside.*] And yet I know not how conceit may rob

The treasury of life when life itself   44

Yields to the theft. Had he been where he thought,

By this had thought been past. Alive or dead?

[*To Gloucester.*] Ho, you, sir! Friend! Hear you, sir?
    Speak!—

Thus might he pass indeed; yet he revives.—   48

What are you, sir?

    Glo.   Away and let me die.

    Edg. Hadst thou been aught but gossamer, feathers, air

(So many fathom down precipitating),

Thou'dst shiver'd like an egg; but thou dost breathe,   52

Hast heavy substance, bleed'st not, speak'st, art sound.

Ten masts at each make not the altitude

Which thou hast perpendicularly fell.

Thy life's a miracle. Speak yet again.   56

    Glo. But have I fallen or no?

    Edg. From the dread summit of this chalky bourn.

Look up a-height! The shrill-gorg'd lark so far

Cannot be seen or heard. Do but look up.   60

    Glo. Alack! I have no eyes.

Is wretchedness depriv'd that benefit

To end itself by death? 'Twas yet some comfort,

When misery could beguile the tyrant's rage,   64

And frustrate his proud will.

---

42 Gone, sir: farewell; *cf. n.*
43–45 conceit . . . theft; *cf. n.*
54 at each: *one on another*
58 summit; *cf. n.*   bourn: *boundary*
59 shrill-gorg'd: *high-voiced*

Edg.   Give me your arm.
Up! So. How is't? Feel you your legs? You stand.

   Glo. Too well, too well.

   Edg.   This is above all strangeness.
Upon the crown o' th' cliff, what thing was that   68
Which parted from you?

   Glo.   A poor unfortunate beggar.

   Edg. As I stood here below, methought his eyes
Were two full moons; he had a thousand noses,
Horns whelk'd and wav'd like the enridged sea.   72
It was some fiend. Therefore, thou happy father,
Think that the clearest gods, who make them honors
Of men's impossibilities, have preserv'd thee.

   Glo. I do remember now. Henceforth I'll bear   76
Affliction till it do cry out itself
'Enough, enough,' and die. That thing you speak of—
I took it for a man—often 'twould say
'The fiend, the fiend.' He led me to that place.   80

   Edg. Bear free and patient thoughts.

Enter Lear, mad.

                         But who comes here?
The safer sense will ne'er accommodate
His master thus.

   Lear. No, they cannot touch me for coining. I am
the king himself.   85

   Edg. O thou side-piercing sight!

   Lear. Nature's above art in that respect. There's

---

72 whelk'd: *twisted*   73 fiend; *cf.* **n.**
74 clearest: *most serene*
82 safer: *saner*   accommodate: *equip*
87 Nature's above art; *cf.* **n.**

your press-money. That fellow handles his bow like
a crow-keeper: draw me a clothier's yard. Look, look!
a mouse. Peace, peace! this piece of toasted cheese
will do't. There's my gauntlet; I'll prove it on a
giant. Bring up the brown bills. O! well flown, bird! I'
the clout, i' the clout: hewgh! Give the word.

Edg. Sweet marjoram.

Lear. Pass.

Glo. I know that voice.   96

Lear. Ha! Goneril, with a white beard! They flatter'd me like a dog, and told me I had white hairs in
my beard ere the black ones were there. To say 'ay'
and 'no' to everything that I said! 'Ay' and 'no' too
was no good divinity. When the rain came to wet me
once and the wind to make me chatter, when the
thunder would not peace at my bidding, there I
found 'em, there I smelt 'em out. Go to! they are not
men o' their words. They told me I was everything.
'Tis a lie: I am not ague-proof.   106

Glo. The trick of that voice I do well remember.
Is't not the king?

Lear.   Ay, every inch a king!
When I do stare, see how the subject quakes.   109

I pardon that man's life. What was thy cause? Adul-

---

88 press-money: *money given to soldiers when pressed into*
   service
89 crow-keeper; *cf. n.* •   clothier's yard: *cloth-yard shaft, used*
   with long bow
92 brown bills: *halberds, or, men carrying them*
93 clout: *bull's-eye, bit of white cloth used for mark in archery*
94 Sweet marjoram; *cf. n.*
98 white hairs: *the marks of wisdom*
100, 101 'Ay' . . . divinity; *cf. n.*
110–127 *Cf. n.*

tery? Thou shalt not die. Die for adultery? No. The wren goes to't, and the small gilded fly does lecher in my sight. Let copulation thrive, for Gloucester's bastard son was kinder to his father than my daughters got 'tween the lawful sheets. To't luxury, pell-mell! for I lack soldiers. Behold yond simpering dame, whose face between her forks presages snow, that minces virtue, and does shake the head to hear of pleasure's name: the fitchew nor the soiled horse goes to't with a more riotous appetite. Down from the waist they are centaurs, though women all above. But to the girdle do the gods inherit, beneath is all the fiends'. There's hell, there's darkness, there is the sulphurous pit: burning, scalding, stench, consumption. Fie, fie, fie! pah, pah! Give me an ounce of civet, good apothecary, to sweeten my imagination. There's money for thee.

Glo. O let me kiss that hand!   128

Lear. Let me wipe it first. It smells of mortality.

Glo. O ruin'd piece of nature! This great world shall so wear out to naught. Do you know me?

Lear. I remember thine eyes well enough. Dost thou squiny at me? No, do thy worst, blind Cupid; I'll not love. Read thou this challenge; mark but the penning of it.

Glo. Were all the letters suns, I could not see.   136

Edg. [*aside*]. I would not take this from report. It is, and my heart breaks at it.

115 luxury: *lewdness*	117 forks: *legs*; cf. *n.*
118 minces: *makes an affected show of*	
119 fitchew: *polecat* soiled: *overfed*	
121 centaurs; cf. *n.*	131 Do you; cf. *n.*
133 squiny: *squint*	134 challenge; cf. *n.*

Lear. Read.

Glo. What! with the case of eyes?   140

Lear. O, ho! are you there with me? No eyes in
your head, nor no money in your purse? Your eyes
are in a heavy case, your purse in a light. Yet you see
how this world goes.   144

Glo. I see it feelingly.

Lear. What! art mad? A man may see how this
world goes with no eyes. Look with thine ears. See
how yond justice rails upon yond simple thief.
Hark, in thine ear: change places, and, handy-dandy,
which is the justice, which is the thief? Thou hast
seen a farmer's dog bark at a beggar?

Glo. Ay, sir.   152

Lear. And the creature run from the cur? There
thou mightst behold the great image of authority: a
dog's obey'd in office.

Thou rascal beadle, hold thy bloody hand!   156
Why dost thou lash that whore? Strip thy own back.
Thou hotly lusts to use her in that kind
For which thou whipp'st her. The usurer hangs the
      cozener.
Through totter'd rags small vices do appear;   160
Robes and furr'd gowns hide all. ⟨Plate sin with gold,
And the strong lance of justice hurtless breaks;
Arm it in rags, a pigmy's straw does pierce it.
None does offend, none, I say none. I'll able 'em.   164

140 case: *sockets*   141 are you . . . me: *so that is it?*
149 handy-dandy; *cf. n.*   155 in office; *cf. n.*
156 beadle: *parish police officer*   158 lusts; *cf. n.*
159 usurer: *rapacious or 'grafting' judge*   cozener: *petty thief*
160 *Cf. n.*
161 Plate sin; *cf. n.*   164 able: *authorize*

Take that of me, my friend, who have the power
To seal th' accuser's lips.⟩ Get thee glass eyes;
And, like a scurvy politician, seem
To see the things thou dost not. Now, now, now, now.
Pull off my boots; harder, harder. So!   169

  Edg. [*aside*]. O matter and impertinency mix'd!
Reason in madness!

  Lear. If thou wilt weep my fortunes, take my eyes.   172
I know thee well enough; thy name is Gloucester.
Thou must be patient; we came crying hither.
Thou know'st the first time that we smell the air
We waul and cry. I will preach to thee: mark.   176

  Glo. Alack! alack the day!

  Lear. When we are born, we cry that we are come
To this great stage of fools. This' a good block!
It were a delicate stratagem to shoe   180
A troop of horse with felt. ⟨I'll put't in proof,⟩
And when I have stol'n upon these son-in-laws,
Then, kill, kill, kill, kill, kill, kill!

Enter three Gentlemen.

  Gent. O here he is! lay hand upon him!—Sir,   184
Your most dear daughter—

  Lear. No rescue? What! a prisoner? I am even
The natural fool of fortune. Use me well;
You shall have ransom. Let me have surgeons;   188
I am cut to th' brains.

  Gent.   You shall have anything.

165 of me: *on my authority*
170 impertinency: *irrelevant talk*
170, 171 O matter . . . madness; *cf. n.*
179 This': *this is*   block: *type of hat; cf. n.*
183 S.d. *Cf. n.*   188 ransom; *cf. n.*

Lear. No seconds? All myself?
Why this would make ⟨a man,⟩ a man of salt,
To use his eyes for garden water-pots,   192
«Ay, and laying autumn's dust.
        Gent.   Good sir,—
        Lear.» I will die bravely like a smug bridegroom.
What! I will be jovial. Come, come! I am a king.
Masters, know you that?   196
Gent. You are a royal one, and we obey you.
        Lear. Then there's life in't. Nay, an you get it,
you shall get it by running. Sa, sa, sa, sa!

                                        Exit King, running.
Gent. A sight most pitiful in the meanest wretch,   200
Past speaking of in a king! Thou hast one daughter,
Who redeems nature from the general curse
Which twain have brought her to.
        Edg. Hail, gentle sir!
        Gent.   Sir, speed you. What's your will?
        Edg. Do you hear aught, sir, of a battle toward? 205
Gent. Most sure and vulgar; every one hears that,
Which can distinguish sound.
        Edg.   But, by your favor,
How near's the other army?   208
Gent. Near, and on speedy foot. The main descry
Stands on the hourly thought.
        Edg.   I thank you, sir: that's all.
        Gent. Though that the queen on special cause is here,
Her army is mov'd on.   *Exit.*

191 man of salt; *cf. n.*   193 Good sir; *cf. n.*
198 life in't: *still hope*   204 speed you: *God prosper you*
206 vulgar: *common*
209 on speedy foot: *approaching fast*   main descry, etc.; *cf. n.*

Edg.   I thank you, sir.   212
Glo. You ever-gentle gods, take my breath from me.
Let not my worser spirit tempt me again
To die before you please.
    Edg.   Well pray you, father.
Glo. Now, good sir, what are you?   216
    Edg. A most poor man, made tame to fortune's blows,
Who, by the art of known and feeling sorrows,
Am pregnant to good pity. Give me your hand,
I'll lead you to some biding.
    Glo.   Hearty thanks.   220
The bounty and the benison of heaven
To boot, and boot!

Enter Steward [Oswald].

    Osw.   A próclaim'd prize! Most happy!
That eyeless head of thine was first fram'd flesh
To raise my fortunes. Thou old unhappy traitor,   224
Briefly thyself remember. The sword is out
That must destroy thee.
    Glo.   Now let thy friendly hand
Put strength enough to't.   [*Edgar interposes.*]
    Osw.   Wherefore, bold peasant,
Dar'st thou support a publish'd traitor? Hence!   228
Lest that th' infection of his fortune take
Like hold on thee. Let go his arm.
    Edg. Chill not let go, zir, without vurther 'casion.
    Osw. Let go, slave, or thou diest.   232

219 pregnant: *ready, receptive*
220 biding: *abiding-place*   222 To boot, and boot; *cf. n.*
225 thyself remember: *think of your sins*
231 Chill: *I will; cf. n.*

Edg. Good gentleman, go your gait, and let poor
volk pass. And chud ha' bin zwaggered out of my life,
'twould not ha' bin zo long as 'tis by a vortnight.
Nay, come not near th' old man. Keep out, che vor ye,
or ise try whether your costard or my batoon be the
harder. Chill be plain with you.   238

Osw. Out, dunghill!

Edg. Chill pick your teeth, zir. Come; no matter
vor your foins.   *They fight.*

Osw. Slave, thou hast slain me. Villain, take my purse.
If ever thou wilt thrive, bury my body;
And give the letters which thou find'st about me   244
To Edmund Earl of Gloucester. Seek him out
Upon the British party. O untimely death!
Death!   *He dies.*

Edg. I know thee well: a serviceable villain,   248
As duteous to the vices of thy mistress
As badness would desire.

Glo.   What! is he dead?

Edg. Sit you down, father; rest you.
Let's see his pockets. These letters that he speaks of 252
May be my friends. He's dead. I am only sorry
He had no other deaths-man. Let us see.—
Leave, gentle wax! and, manners, blame us not.
To know our enemies' minds, we rip their hearts;   256
Their papers, is more lawful.   *Reads the letter.*

234 And chud: *if I should*
236 che vor ye: *I warn you; cf. n.*
237 costard: *apple, used jokingly for head*   batoon: *cudgel*
                                                      cf. n.
241 foins: *thrusts*
246 British party; *cf. n.*   255 Leave: *give leave*

Let our reciprocal vows be remembered. You have many
opportunities to cut him off. If your will want not, time and
place will be fruitfully offered. There is nothing done if he
return the conqueror. Then am I the prisoner, and his bed
my gaol, from the loathed warmth whereof deliver me, and
supply the place for your labor.

Your wife (so I would say), your affectionate servant,
«and for you her own tormenter,»

                                              Goneril.

O undistinguish'd space of woman's will!
A plot upon her virtuous husband's life,   268
And the exchange my brother! Here, in the sands,
Thee I'll rake up, the post unsanctified
Of murtherous lechers; and in the mature time
With this ungracious paper strike the sight   272
Of the death-practis'd duke. For him 'tis well
That of thy death and business I can tell.
   Glo. The king is mad. How stiff is my vile sense,
That I stand up, and have ingenious feeling   276
Of my huge sorrows! Better I were distract.
So should my thoughts be fenced from my griefs,
And woes by wrong imaginations lose
The knowledge of themselves.   *A drum afar off.*
   Edg.   Give me your hand!   280
Far off, methinks, I hear the beaten drum.
Come, father, I'll bestow you with a friend.   *Exeunt.*

259 want not: *be not wanting*
265 and . . . tormenter; *cf. n.*
267 undistinguish'd space: *incalculable scope*
270 rake up: *cover*
271 in . . . time: *when the time is ripe*
273 death-practis'd: *mortally plotted against*
275 stiff: *tough*
276 ingenious: *conscious*   278 fenced; *cf. n.*

SCENE SEVENTH

[A Tent in the French Camp]

Enter Cordelia, Kent, and Doctor [with a Gentleman].

Cor. O thou good Kent! how shall I live and work
To match thy goodness? My life will be too short,
And every measure fail me.

    Kent. To be acknowledg'd, madam, is o'erpaid.   4
All my reports go with the modest truth,
Nor more nor clipp'd, but so.

    Cor.   Be better suited.
These weeds are memories of those worser hours.
I prithee, put them off.

    Kent.   Pardon me, dear madam.   8
Yet to be known shortens my made intent.
My boon I make it that you know me not
Till time and I think meet.

    Cor. Then be't so, my good lord.—*[To the Doctor.]*
    How does the king?   12

    Doct. Madam, sleeps still.

    Cor.   O you kind gods,
Cure this great breach in his abused nature!
Th' untun'd and jarring senses O wind up
Of this child-changed father!

Scene Seventh. *Cf. n.*   5 modest: *measured*
6 Nor . . . clipp'd: *neither exaggerated nor palliated*   Be
   better suited: *dress yourself more suitably to your rank*
7 weeds: *clothes*   9 made intent: *fixed purpose*   yet . . .
   intent; *cf. n.*
10 My boon I make it: *I ask as a favor*
16 child-changed; *cf. n.*

Doct.   So please your majesty   16
That we may wake the king? He hath slept long.

Cor. Be govern'd by your knowledge, and proceed
I' th' sway of your own will. Is he array'd?

Doct. Ay, madam; in the heaviness of sleep,   20
We put fresh garments on him.

Enter Lear in a chair carried by Servants.

Be by, good madam, when we do awake him;
I doubt not of his temperance.

«*Cor.*   Very well.

Doct. Please you, draw near. Louder the music there.»

Cor. O my dear father! Restoration, hang   25
Thy medicine on my lips, and let this kiss
Repair those violent harms that my two sisters
Have in thy reverence made!

Kent.   Kind and dear princess! 28

Cor. Had you not been their father, these white flakes
Had challeng'd pity of them. Was this a face
To be expos'd against the warring winds?
«To stand against the deep dread-bolted thunder   32
In the most terrible and nimble stroke
Of quick cross lightning? to watch—poor pérdu!—
With this thin helm?» Mine enemy's dog,
Though he had bit me, should have stood that night   36
Against my fire. And wast thou fain, poor father,
To hovel thee with swine and rogues forlorn
In short and musty straw? Alack! alack!

---

23 temperance: *mental balance*   29 flakes: *locks of hair*
30, 31 Was . . . winds; *cf. n.*
34 pérdu: *soldier on detached and dangerous sentry duty*
35 this thin helm: *only his bare skull*

'Tis wonder that thy life and wits at once   40
Had not concluded all. He wakes. Speak to him.

   Doct. Madam, do you; 'tis fittest.

   Cor. How does my royal lord? How fares your majesty?

   Lear. You do me wrong to take me out o' th' grave.   44
Thou art a soul in bliss; but I am bound
Upon a wheel of fire, that mine own tears
Do scald like molten lead.

   Cor.   Sir, do you know me?

   Lear. You are a spirit, I know. Where did you die?   48

   Cor. Still, still, far wide.

   Doct. He's scarce awake. Let him alone awhile.

   Lear. Where have I been? Where am I? Fair daylight!
I am mightily abus'd. I should e'en die with pity   52
To see another thus. I know not what to say.
I will not swear these are my hands. Let's see.
I feel this pin prick. Would I were assur'd
Of my condition!

   Cor.   O look upon me, sir,   56
And hold your hands in benediction o'er me.
«No, sir,» you must not kneel.

   Lear.   Pray, do not mock me.
I am a very foolish fond old man,
Fourscore and upward, ⟨not an hour more nor less;⟩   60
And to deal plainly,
I fear I am not in my perfect mind.
Methinks I should know you and know this man;
Yet I am doubtful, for I am mainly ignorant   64
What place this is, and all the skill I have
Remembers not these garments; nor I know not

41 all: *entirely*
46 that: *so that*   64 mainly: *mightily*

Where I did lodge last night. Do not laugh at me;
For, as I am a man, I think this lady　　68
To be my child Cordelia.
　　Cor.　　　　　　　　　And so I am, ⟨I am.⟩
　　Lear. Be your tears wet? Yes, faith. I pray, weep not.
If you have poison for me, I will drink it.
I know you do not love me, for your sisters　　72
Have (as I do remember) done me wrong.
You have some cause, they have not.
　　Cor.　　　　　　　　　No cause, no cause.
　　Lear. Am I in France?
　　Kent.　　　　　　　In your own kingdom, sir.
　　Lear. Do not abuse me.　　76
　　Doct. Be comforted, good madam. The great rage,
You see, is cur'd in him «and yet it is danger
To make him even o'er the time he has lost.»
Desire him to go in; trouble him no more　　80
Till further settling.
　　Cor. Will't please your highness walk?
　　Lear.　　　　　　　You must bear with me.
Pray you now, forget and forgive. I am old and foolish.
　　　　　　　　　　Exeunt. Manent Kent and Gent.
　　«*Gent.* Holds it true, sir, that the Duke of Corn-
wall was so slain?　　85
　　Kent. Most certain, sir.
　　Gent. Who is conductor of his people?
　　Kent. As 'tis said, the bastard son of Gloucester.　　88
　　Gent. They say Edgar, his banished son, is with
the Earl of Kent in Germany.
　　Kent. Report is changeable. 'Tis time to look about;
the powers of the kingdom approach apace.　　92

78 cur'd; *cf. n.*　　　　79 even o'er: *smooth out, clear up*

Gent. The arbitrement is like to be bloody. Fare
you well, sir.   [*Exit.*]

Kent. My point and period will be throughly wrought,
Or well or ill, as this day's battle's fought.   *Exit.*»

ACT FIFTH

SCENE FIRST

[*The British Camp near Dover*]

Enter, with drum and colors, Edmund, Regan,
Gentlemen, and Soldiers.

Edm. Know of the duke if his last purpose hold,
Or whether since he is advis'd by aught
To change the course. He's full of alteration
And self-reproving. Bring his constant pleasure.   4
                                    [*To one, who goes out.*]

Reg. Our sister's man is certainly miscarried.
Edm. 'Tis to be doubted, madam.
Reg.   Now, sweet lord,
You know the goodness I intend upon you.
Tell me, but truly, but then speak the truth,   8
Do you not love my sister?
Edm.   In honor'd love.
Reg. But have you never found my brother's way
To the forefended place?

93 arbitrement: *process of decision*   4 constant: *settled*
6 doubted: *feared*   11 forefended: *forbidden*

«*Edm.*   That thought abuses you.

Reg. I am doubtful that you have been conjunct   12
And bosom'd with her, as far as we call hers.»

Edm. No, by mine honor, madam.

Reg. I never shall endure her. Dear my lord,
Be not familiar with her.

Edm.   Fear «me» not.   16
She and the duke her husband!

*Enter with drum and colors, Albany,
Goneril, Soldiers.*

«*Gon.* [*aside*]. I had rather lose the battle than that
    sister
Should loosen him and me.»

Alb. Our very loving sister, well be-met.   20
Sir, this I heard, the king is come to his daughter,
With others whom the rigor of our state
Forc'd to cry out. «Where I could not be honest
I never yet was valiant. For this business,   24
It touches us, as France invades our land,
Not bolds the king, with others whom, I fear,
Most just and heavy causes make oppose.

Edm. Sir, you speak nobly.»

Reg.   Why is this reason'd?   28

Gon. Combine together 'gainst the enemy,
For these domestic poor particulars
Are not to question here.

Alb.   Let's then determine

12, 13 conjunct and bosom'd: *united and intimate*
13 as far . . . hers; *cf. n.*   16 Fear: *doubt*
24 For: *as for*   26 Not bolds, etc.; *cf. n.*
28 reason'd: *discussed*   30, 31 For . . . here; *cf. n.*

With th' ancient of war on our proceeding.   32
    «*Edm.* I shall attend you presently at your tent.»
    Reg. Sister, you'll go with us?
    Gon. No.
    Reg. 'Tis most convenient. Pray you, go with us.   36
    Gon. [*aside*]. O, ho! I know the riddle. [*Aloud.*] I will
        go.   *Exeunt both the Armies.*

Enter Edgar.

    Edg. If e'er your Grace had speech with man so poor,
Hear me one word.
    Alb.   I'll overtake you.—Speak.
                    Exeunt [*Edmund, Regan, Goneril*].
    Edg. Before you fight the battle, ope this letter.   40
If you have victory, let the trumpet sound
For him that brought it. Wretched though I seem,
I can produce a champion that will prove
What is avouched there. If you miscarry,   44
Your business of the world hath so an end,
⟨And machination ceases.⟩ Fortune love you!
    Alb. Stay till I have read the letter.
    Edg.   I was forbid it.
When time shall serve, let but the herald cry,   48
And I'll appear again.   *Exit.*
    Alb. Why, fare thee well. I will o'erlook thy paper.

Enter Edmund.

    Edm. The enemy's in view; draw up your powers.
Here is the guess of their true strength and forces   52

32 ancient of war: *veteran soldiers*
36 convenient: *proper, convenable*
37 riddle; *cf. n.*   44 avouched: *asserted*

By diligent discovery; but your haste
Is now urg'd on you.

   Alb.   We will greet the time.   *Exit.*

   Edm. To both these sisters have I sworn my love,
Each jealous of the other as the stung   56
Are of the adder. Which of them shall I take?
Both? one? or neither? Neither can be enjoy'd
If both remain alive. To take the widow
Exasperates, makes mad, her sister Goneril;   60
And hardly shall I carry out my side,
Her husband being alive. Now then, we'll use
His countenance for the battle; which being done
Let her who would be rid of him devise   64
His speedy taking off. As for the mercy
Which he intends to Lear and to Cordelia,
The battle done, and they within our power,
Shall never see his pardon; for my state   68
Stands on me to defend, not to debate.   *Exit.*

53 discovery: *reconnoitring; cf. n.*   54 time: *occasion*
56 jealous: *suspicious*
61 carry . . . side: *play out my game*   68 Shall: *they shall*
69 Stands on me: *it is important for me*

SCENE SECOND

[*A Field between the two Camps*]

*Alarum. Enter the powers of France over the stage, Cor-
delia with her father in her hand, and exeunt. Enter
Edgar and Gloucester.*

Edg. Here, father, take the shadow of this bush
For your good host; pray that the right may thrive.
If ever I return to you again,
I'll bring you comfort.
   Glo.   Grace go with you, sir!   4
                                      Exit [*Edgar*].

Alarum and Retreat within. Enter Edgar.

   Edg. Away, old man! give me thy hand. Away!
King Lear hath lost, he and his daughter ta'en.
Give me thy hand. Come on.
   Glo. No farther, sir. A man may rot even here.   8
   Edg. What! in ill thoughts again? Men must endure
Their going hence, even as their coming hither.
Ripeness is all. Come on.
   ⟨*Glo.*   And that's true too.⟩   *Exeunt.*

Scene Second. S.d. *in her hand*: his hand clasped in hers; *cf. n.*
1 bush; *cf. n.*   11 Ripeness: *readiness; cf. n.*

SCENE THIRD

[The British Camp, near Dover]

Enter, in conquest, with drum and colors, Edmund; Lear and Cordelia as prisoners, Soldiers, Captain.

Edm. Some officers take them away! Good guard,
Until their greater pleasures first be known
That are to censure them.

   Cor.   We are not the first
Who, with best meaning, have incurr'd the worst.   4
For thee, oppressed king, I am cast down;
Myself could else out-frown false Fortune's frown.
Shall we not see these daughters and these sisters?

   Lear. No, no ⟨, no, no⟩! Come, let's away to prison.   8
We two alone will sing like birds i' th' cage.
When thou dost ask me blessing, I'll kneel down,
And ask of thee forgiveness. So we'll live,
And pray, and sing, and tell old tales, and laugh   12
At gilded butterflies, and hear poor rogues
Talk of court news; and we'll talk with them too:
Who loses and who wins, who's in, who's out;
And take upon's the mystery of things,   16
As if we were God's spies; and we'll wear out,
In a wall'd prison, packs and sects of great ones
That ebb and flow by th' moon.

   Edm.   Take them away.

   Lear. Upon such sacrifices, my Cordelia,   20

Scene Third. S.d. *Cf. n.*   1 Good guard: *guard them well*
2 their greater pleasures; *cf. n.*   16, 17 *Cf. n.*
18 packs and sects; *cf. n.*   20 sacrifices: *i.e., of liberty; cf. n.*

The gods themselves throw incense. Have I caught thee?
He that parts us shall bring a brand from heaven,
And fire us hence like foxes. Wipe thine eyes.
The good years shall devour them, flesh and fell,   2.
Ere they shall make us weep. We'll see 'em starv'd first.
Come.   *Exit [with Cordelia, guarded]*

    Edm. Come hither, captain; hark.
Take thou this note. [*Gives a paper.*] Go follow them to
    prison.   2\
One step I have advanc'd thee. If thou dost
As this instructs thee, thou dost make thy way
To noble fortunes. Know thou this, that men
Are as the time is; to be tender-minded   3\
Does not become a sword. Thy great employment
Will not bear question. Either say thou'lt do't,
Or thrive by other means.

    Capt.   I'll do't, my lord.
    Edm. About it; and write happy when thou'st done. 3(
Mark! I say, instantly, and carry it so
As I have set it down.

    «*Capt.* I cannot draw a cart nor eat dried oats.
If it be man's work I'll do't.»   *Exit Captain*

    Flourish. Enter Albany, Goneril, Regan, Soldiers.

    Alb. Sir, you have show'd to-day your valiant strain, 4
And fortune led you well. You have the captives
Who were the opposites of this day's strife.

22, 23 He . . . foxes; *cf. n.*
24 good years; *cf. n.*   fell: *skin*
33, 34 Thy . . . question; *cf. n.*
36 write happy: *call yourself lucky*
39 *Cf. n.*   40 man's work: *anything a man can d*
40 S.d. *Cf. n.*   42 led you well: *was good to yo*

do require them of you, so to use them   44
As we shall find their merits and our safety
May equally determine.

 Edm.   Sir, I thought it fit
To send the old and miserable king
To some retention «and appointed guard»,   48
Whose age has charms in it, whose title more,
To pluck the common bosom on his side,
And turn our ímpress'd lances in our eyes
Which do command them. With him I sent the queen—
My reason all the same; and they are ready   53
To-morrow, or at further space, t'appear
Where you shall hold your session. «At this time
We sweat and bleed, the friend hath lost his friend;   56
And the best quarrels in the heat are curs'd
By those that feel their sharpness.
The question of Cordelia and her father
Requires a fitter place.»

 Alb.   Sir, by your patience,   60
I hold you but a subject of this war,
Not as a brother.

 Reg.   That's as we list to grace him.
Methinks our pleasure might have been demanded,
Ere you had spoke so far. He led our powers,   64
Bore the commission of my place and person;
The which immediacy may well stand up,
And call itself your brother.

 Gon.   Not so hot!

44 I; *cf. n.*   48 retention: *detention*
50 common bosom: *affection of the populace*
51 impress'd: *enlisted*   57, 58 *Cf. n.*
63 demanded: *inquired*
66 immediacy: *position as my direct agent*

In his own grace he doth exalt himself   68
More than in your addition.

    Reg.   In my rights,
By me invested, he compeers the best.

    Alb. That were the most, if he should husband you.

    Reg. Jesters do oft prove prophets.

    Gon.   Holla, holla!   72
That eye that told you so look'd but a-squint.

    Reg. Lady, I am not well; else I should answer
From a full-flowing stomach. General,
Take thou my soldiers, prisoners, patrimony.   76
(Dispose of them, of me; the whole is thine.)
Witness the world, that I create thee here
My lord and master.

    Gon.   Mean you to enjoy him?

    Alb. The let-alone lies not in your good will.   80

    Edm. Nor in thine, lord.

    Alb.   Half-blooded fellow, yes.

    Reg. [*to Edmund*]. Let the drum strike, and prove my
    title thine.

    Alb. Stay yet. Hear reason. Edmund, I arrest thee
On capital treason; and, in thine attaint,   84
This gilded serpent [*pointing to Goneril*]. For your claim,
    fair sister,
I bar it in the interest of my wife.
'Tis she is sub-contracted to this lord,
And I, her husband, contradict your bans.   88
If you will marry, make your love to me;

69 your addition; *cf. n.*   70 compeers: *equals*
71 the most: *the most he could claim; cf. n.*
75 stomach: *passion*
77 *Cf. n.*   80 let-alone: *quit-claim; cf. n.*
82 *Cf. n.*   84 attaint; *cf. n.*

My lady is bespoke.

  ⟨*Gon.*   An interlude!

  Alb.⟩ Thou art arm'd, Gloucester. ⟨Let the trumpet
    sound.⟩

If none appear to prove upon thy person   92

Thy heinous, manifest, and many treasons,

There is my pledge! [*Throws down a glove.*] I'll mark it
    on thy heart,

Ere I taste bread, thou art in nothing less

Than I have here proclaim'd thee.

  Reg.   Sick! O sick!   96

  Gon. [*aside*]. If not, I'll ne'er trust medicine.

  Edm. There's my exchange. [*Throws down a glove.*]
    What in the world he is

That names me traitor, villain-like he lies.

Call by thy trumpet. He that dares approach,   100

On him, on you—who not?—I will maintain

My truth and honor firmly.

  Alb. A herald, ho!

  «*Edm.*   A herald, ho! a herald!

  Alb.» Trust to thy single virtue; for thy soldiers,   104

All levied in my name, have in my name

Took their discharge.

  Reg.   My sickness grows upon me.

  Alb. She is not well. Convey her to my tent.

                        [*Exit Regan, led.*]

Enter a Herald.

Come hither, herald. Let the trumpet sound,   108

And read out this.

90 An interlude: *'This is as good as a play'*
94 mark; *cf. n.*   104 single virtue: *unaided valor*

«*Capt.* Sound, trumpet!»   *A trumpet sounds*

Herald reads.

If any man of quality or degree within the lists of the
army will maintain upon Edmund, supposed Earl of
Gloucester, that he is a manifold traitor, let him appear
by the third sound of the trumpet. He is bold in his defence.

«*Edm.* Sound!»   *1 Trumpet*
Her. Again!   *2 Trumpet*
Her. Again!   *3 Trumpet*
                          Trumpet answers within

Enter Edgar, armed, at the third sound, a trumpet
before him.

Alb. Ask him his purposes, why he appears
Upon this call o' th' trumpet.
     Her.   What are you?
Your name? your quality? and why you answer   12(
This present summons?
     Edg.   Know, my name is lost,
By treason's tooth bare-gnawn and canker-bit.
Yet am I noble as the adversary
I come to cope.
     Alb.   Which is that adversary?   12
     Edg. What's he that speaks for Edmund Earl o
     Gloucester?
     Edm. Himself. What sayst thou to him?
     Edg.   Draw thy sword
That, if my speech offend a noble heart,

111 lists: *limits, borders*
112 supposed: *putative, soi-disant*
117 S.d. trumpet: *trumpeter*
122 canker-bit: *worm-eaten*   124 cope: *mee*

Thy arm may do thee justice. Here is mine: 128
Behold, it is the privilege of my tongue,
My oath, and my profession. I protest,
Maugre thy strength, youth, place, and eminence,
Despite thy victor sword and fire-new fortune,   132
Thy valor and thy heart, thou art a traitor,
False to thy gods, thy brother, and thy father,
Conspirant 'gainst this high illustrious prince,
And, from th' extremest upward of thy head   136
To the descent and dust beneath thy feet,
A most toad-spotted traitor. Say thou 'No,'
This sword, this arm, and my best spirits are bent
To prove upon thy heart, whereto I speak,   140
Thou liest.

   Edm.   In wisdom I should ask thy name;
But since thy outside looks so fair and warlike,
And that thy tongue some say of breeding breathes,
(What safe and nicely I might well delay)   144
By rule of knighthood, I disdain and spurn.
Back do I toss those treasons to thy head,
With the hell-hated lie o'erwhelm thy heart,
Which, for they yet glance by and scarcely bruise,   148
This sword of mine shall give them instant way,
Where they shall rest for ever. Trumpets, speak!

               Alarums. Fights. [Edmund falls.]

   Alb. Save him, save him!

   Gon.   This is mere practice, Gloucester.

---

128 mine: *my sword*   129 privilege: *warrant; cf. n.*
131 Maugre: *despite*
137 descent and dust: *dusty depth (hendiadys)*
143 say: *smack, hint*
144 safe and nicely: *prudently and fastidiously; cf. n.*
146, 147 treasons, lie; *cf. n.*

By th' law of arms thou wast not bound to answer   152
An unknown opposite. Thou art not vanquish'd,
But cozen'd and beguil'd.

Alb.   Stop your mouth, dame,
Or with this paper shall I stopple it. ⟨Hold, sir.⟩
Thou worse than any name, read thine own evil.—   156
No tearing, lady; I perceive you know it.

Gon. Say, if I do. The laws are mine, not thine.
Who can arraign me for't?

Alb.   Most monstrous!
Know'st thou this paper?

Gon.   Ask me not what I know.   160
                              Exit Goneril.

Alb. Go after her. She's desperate; govern her.
                              [*Exit an Officer.*]

Edm. What you have charg'd me with, that have I done,
And more, much more. The time will bring it out.
'Tis past, and so am I. But what art thou   164
That hast this fortune on me? If thou'rt noble,
I do forgive thee.

Edg.   Let's exchange charity.
I am no less in blood than thou art, Edmund;
If more, the more thou'st wrong'd me.   168
My name is Edgar, and thy father's son.
The gods are just, and of our pleasant vices
Make instruments to plague us:
The dark and vicious place where thee he got   172
Cost him his eyes.

Edm.   Thou'st spoken right. 'Tis true.

154, 155 Stop . . . it; *cf. n.*
155 stopple: *close as with a bung or cork*
160 Ask . . . know; *cf. n.*

The wheel is come full circle; I am here.

   Alb. Methought thy very gait did prophesy

A royal nobleness. I must embrace thee.   176

Let sorrow split my heart, if ever I

Did hate thee or thy father.

   Edg.   Worthy prince, I know't.

   Alb. Where have you hid yourself?

How have you known the miseries of your father?   180

   Edg. By nursing them, my lord. List a brief tale;

And, when 'tis told, O that my heart would burst!

The bloody proclamation to escape

That follow'd me so near—(O our lives' sweetness!   184

That we the pain of death would hourly die

Rather than die at once!)—taught me to shift

Into a madman's rags, t'assume a semblance

That very dogs disdain'd: and in this habit   188

Met I my father with his bleeding rings,

Their precious stones new lost; became his guide,

Led him, begg'd for him, sav'd him from despair;

Never, (O fault!) reveal'd myself unto him,   192

Until some half hour past, when I was arm'd,

Not sure, though hoping, of this good success.

I ask'd his blessing, and from first to last

Told him my pilgrimage; but his flaw'd heart   196

(Alack! too weak the conflict to support)

'Twixt two extremes of passion, joy and grief,

Burst smilingly.

   Edm.   This speech of yours hath mov'd me,

And shall perchance do good; but speak you on.   200

You look as you had something more to say.

---

174 I am here; *cf. n.*   183 *Cf. n.*

189 rings: *eye-sockets*

Alb. If there be more, more woeful, hold it in;
For I am almost ready to dissolve,
Hearing of this.

   «*Edg.*   This would have seem'd a period   204
To such as love not sorrow; but another
To amplify too much, would make much more,
And top extremity. Whilst I was big
In clamor came there in a man,   208
Who, having seen me in my worst estate,
Shunn'd my abhorr'd society; but then, finding
Who 'twas that so endur'd, with his strong arms
He fasten'd on my neck, and bellow'd out   212
As he'd burst heaven; threw him on my father,
Told the most piteous tale of Lear and him
That ever ear receiv'd; which in recounting
His grief grew puissant, and the strings of life   216
Began to crack. Twice then the trumpets sounded,
And there I left him tranc'd.

   Alb.   But who was this?

   Edg. Kent, sir, the banish'd Kent; who in disguise
Follow'd his enemy king, and did him service   220
Improper for a slave.»

Enter a Gentleman with a bloody knife.

   Gent. Help, help! O help!

   Edg.   What kind of help?

   ⟨*Alb.*   Speak, **man**.

   Edg.⟩ What means this bloody knife?

---

204 period: *full stop (the ultimate)*
205–207 but another . . . extremity; *cf. n.*
209, 210 having . . . society; *cf. n.*
213 threw him; *cf. n.*

                                222 Cf. *n.*

Gent.   'Tis hot, it smokes;
It came even from the heart of—⟨O! she's dead.⟩   224
   Alb. Who dead? speak, man.
   Gent. Your lady, sir, your lady; and her sister
By her is poison'd. She confesses it.
   Edm. I was contracted to them both. All three   228
Now marry in an instant.
   Edg.   Here comes Kent, sir.

Enter Kent.

   Alb. Produce the bodies, be they alive or dead.
This judgment of the heavens, that makes us tremble,
Touches us not with pity. [*To Kent.*]
                             O! is this he?
The time will not allow the compliment   233
Which very manners urges.
   Kent.   I am come
To bid my king and master aye good-night;
Is he not here?
   Alb.   Great thing of us forgot!   236
Speak, Edmund, where's the king? and where's Cordelia?
      The bodies of Goneril and Regan are brought in.
Seest thou this object, Kent?
   Kent.   Alack! why thus?
   Edm. Yet Edmund was belov'd. The one the other
Poison'd for my sake, and after slew herself.   240
   Alb. Even so. Cover their faces.
   Edm. I pant for life. Some good I mean to do
Despite of mine own nature. Quickly send,
⟨Be brief in it!⟩ to th' castle, for my writ   244

229 Cf. *n.*   235 aye: *forever*
240 Cf. *n.*   244 brief: *hasty*   castle: *Dover Castle*

Is on the life of Lear and on Cordelia.
Nay, send in time.

    Alb.   Run, run! O run!

    Edg. To who, my lord? [*To Edmund.*] Who has the
    office? Send
Thy token of reprieve.

    Edm.   Well thought on. Take my sword,
Give it the captain.

    Alb.   Haste thee, for thy life.

                       [*Exit Edgar.*]

    Edm. He hath commission from thy wife and me
To hang Cordelia in the prison, and
To lay the blame upon her own despair,   252
That she fordid herself.

    Alb. The gods defend her! Bear him hence awhile.

               [*Edmund is borne off.*]

*Enter Lear, with Cordelia in his arms [followed by
    Edgar, Captain, and others].*

    Lear. Howl, howl, howl, howl! O, you are men of
    stones!
Had I your tongues and eyes, I'd use them so   256
That heaven's vault should crack. She's gone for ever.
I know when one is dead, and when one lives.
She's dead as earth. Lend me a looking-glass.
If that her breath will mist or stain the stone,   260
Why, then she lives.

    Kent.   Is this the promis'd end?

    Edg. Or image of that horror.

    Alb.   Fall and cease!

253 fordid: *slew*
260 stone: *mirror*   261 end: *Judgment Day*
262 Or image: *It is, or else the image*   Fall and cease; *cf. n.*

Lear. This feather stirs; she lives! If it be so,
It is a chance which does redeem all sorrows   264
That ever I have felt.

Kent.   O, my good master!

Lear. Prithee, away.

Edg.   'Tis noble Kent, your friend.

Lear. A plague upon you, murderers, traitors all!
I might have sav'd her; now, she's gone for ever!   268
Cordelia, Cordelia! stay a little. Ha!
What is't thou sayst? Her voice was ever soft,
Gentle, and low, an excellent thing in woman.
I kill'd the slave that was a-hanging thee.   272

Capt. 'Tis true, my lords, he did.

Lear.   Did I not, fellow?
I have seen the day, with my good biting falchion
I would have made them skip. I am old now,
And these same crosses spoil me. Who are you?   276
Mine eyes are not o' th' best. I'll tell you straight.

Kent. If fortune brag of two she lov'd and hated,
One of them we behold.

Lear. ⟨This is a dull sight.⟩ Are you not Kent?

Kent.   The same,   280
Your servant Kent. Where is your servant Caius?

Lear. He's a good fellow, I can tell you that.
He'll strike, and quickly too. He's dead and rotten.

Kent. No, my good lord. I am the very man—   284

Lear. I'll see that straight.

274, 275 I have . . . skip; *cf. n.*   274 falchion: *broad sword*
276 these same crosses: *all these adversities*
277 tell you straight: *recognize you in a moment*
278, 279 *Cf. n.*
280 This . . . sight: *'My eyes are certainly bad'*
285 I'll . . . straight: *you must prove that to me at once*

Kent. That, from your first of difference and decay,
Have follow'd your sad steps.

    Lear.   You are welcome hither.

    Kent. Nor no man else. All's cheerless, dark, and
    deadly.   288
Your eldest daughters have fordone themselves,
And desperately are dead.

    Lear.   Ay, so I think.

    Alb. He knows not what he says, and vain is it
That we present us to him.

    Edg.   Very bootless.   292

Enter a Messenger.

    Mess. Edmund is dead, my lord.

    Alb.   That's but a trifle here.
You lords and noble friends, know our intent:
What comfort to this great decay may come
Shall be applied. For us, we will resign,   296
During the life of this old majesty,
To him our absolute power.—[*To Edgar and Kent.*] You,
    to your rights,
With boot and such addition as your honors
Have more than merited. All friends shall taste   300
The wages of their virtue, and all foes
The cup of their deservings. O! see, see!

    Lear. And my poor fool is hang'd! No, no, no life!
Why should a dog, a horse, a rat, have life,   304
And thou no breath at all? Thou'lt come no more.

---

286 your first . . . decay: *the beginning of your friction and*
    misfortune
288 Nor . . . else; *cf. n.*   294 know our intent; *cf. n.*
298 You . . . rights; *cf. n.*   303 fool; *cf. n.*

Never, never, never, never, never!
Pray you, undo this button. Thank you, sir.
⟨Do you see this? Look on her! look! her lips!   308
Look there, look there!⟩ «O, O, O, O.»   *He dies.*

   Edg.   He faints!—My lord, my lord!

   Kent. Break, heart. I prithee, break.

   Edg.   Look up, my lord.

   Kent. Vex not his ghost. O let him pass! He hates him
That would upon the rack of this tough world   312
Stretch him out longer.

   Edg.   He is gone, indeed.

   Kent. The wonder is he hath endur'd so long.
He but usurp'd his life.

   Alb. Bear them from hence. Our present business   316
Is general woe. [*To Kent and Edgar.*] Friends of my soul,
     you twain
Rule in this realm, and the gor'd state sustain.

   Kent. I have a journey, sir, shortly to go.
My master calls me. I must not say no.   320

   Edg. The weight of this sad time we must obey;
Speak what we feel, not what we ought to say.
The oldest hath borne most: we that are young
Shall never see so much, nor live so long.   324

                   Exeunt, with a dead march.

315 usurp'd: *retained against natural law*
321 *Edg.* Cf. *n.*

FINIS

NOTES

At the time of his sudden death in June of 1946, Professor Brooke had completed his work on the text, notes, and glosses for Hamlet, King Lear, Othello and I Henry IV. The editorial tasks which he left unfinished—preparation of some of the final copy for the press, reading of the proofs, compilation of the Indexes of Words Glossed, decisions as to certain matters of style and format, and, in the case of I Henry IV, the rescuing of the text from the prescriptive punctuation of the eighteenth-century editors—have been undertaken by Professor Benjamin Nangle.

TEXTUAL NOTE. The two authorities for the text of *King Lear* are the version included in the first folio (collected) edition of Shakespeare's dramatic works, published in 1623, and the first quarto (separate) edition, printed in 1608 and advertised on the titlepage for sale 'at the signe of the Pide Bull.' The quarto reprint of this (Q 2), which claims the same date on its titlepage but was produced over ten years later, has only very occasional textual significance. There is no good ground for doubting that Shakespeare wrote every line of *King Lear* to be found in the modern 'conflated' texts, though these contain more than was printed in any single early edition (see note on III.ii.79–96). The first Quarto preserves some three hundred lines which the Folio omitted; these, in the present book, are printed within ornamental brackets (« »). On the other hand, the Quarto omits about a hundred lines found in the Folio, which are here placed within angle brackets (⟨ ⟩). Thus about an eighth of the play is found in one or other of the original texts, but not in both. For the remainder there is no doubt that the Folio is in general the better and safer guide; but in recent years the Quarto has been unduly disparaged.

Very eminent authorities have condemned it as a 'reported' text, made up either from the recollection of actors who had played in *Lear* or from shorthand notes taken during a performance. The same authorities have, on the other hand, given countenance to a theory, proposed by P. A. Daniel in 1885, that the good Folio text was set up from a copy of this same bad Quarto which had been corrected by collation with the theatre manuscript of the play. The two assumptions, which are rather inconsistent with each other, combine to produce the allegation that neither of the two fundamental texts of *King Lear* was printed from a *bona fide* manuscript, and such a conclusion would put the textual integrity of the play as it has come down to us under very grave suspicion. There seems, however, to be no substantial evidence for either of the underlying assumptions.

The Quarto is much too good to be a reported text. Though it abounds in slovenliness of various kinds, it presents a very full and essentially faithful version of the play, such as would be produced by a printer struggling honestly (however ineffectually at times) with a difficult handwriting and yet more difficult style. The two most glaring faults, which have done much to injure its reputation, are its frequent inability to distinguish verse from prose and its scandalously light punctuation. Except at the ends of speeches it uses few stops beyond commas, and runs sentences together in a most abandoned way. Of the lines which are properly blank verse, the Quarto sets up five hundred as plain prose and mis-divides a couple of hundred others. (See Edward Hubler, 'The Verse Lining of the First Quarto of *King Lear*,' *Parrott Presentation Volume*, 1935, 421–441.)

For these things Shakespeare was largely to blame. His remarkably flexible and sinuous blank verse in *Lear*, his habit of beginning and ending speeches in the middle of lines, and of mingling prose and poetry without warning in the same scene make the division of a passage into its constituent verse units, once the visual distinction has been obscured, a work for none but a trained prosodist. The Folio, though based on a much clearer manuscript, makes many errors of this kind, and the editors of the play have continued through the centuries to make some (see note on IV.vi.110–127). The very badness of the Quarto in these respects is, in the circumstances, rather a testimony of authenticity, for it is not likely that any one but the poet himself would have produced a manuscript as disorderly as the one from which the first Quarto was evidently printed. It must have been a manuscript in which margins and capitalization were so disregarded that verse and prose looked alike, and in which punctuation and legibility were at a minimum. Within two years after the writing of the play no such manuscript is likely to have been in existence except the author's 'foul papers' or personal draft, and it may be surmised that *King Lear* first got into print as a result of the same haul by Thomas Thorpe and his gang which in the next year, 1609, led to the equally unauthorized publication of the *Sonnets* and *Troilus and Cressida*.

The Quarto compositor found his manuscript hard to read and sometimes blundered, or was stopped dead by an illegibility. As is well known, over a hundred of these faults were discovered while the sheets were being printed, and somebody in the printing house corrected or attempted to correct them. (See W. W. Greg, *The Variants in the First Quarto of 'King Lear,'* 1940.) Often, especially when printing verse as prose and therefore deprived of the check of rhythm, the compositor allowed small words to drop out or get transposed, and sometimes he 'vulgarized,' that is, simplified or paraphrased. These are mainly errors imposed upon him by the difficulty of his 'copy.' But not infrequently he rose above them and came almost as near perfection as the text of *Lear* can come. In Lear's long and passionate speech, 'O reason not the need!' (II.iv.265–287), the Quarto agrees with the Folio altogether in line arrangement and varies in wording in only six cases, one of which is a clear (though slight) Folio error. In Lear's shorter speech, 'Poor naked wretches, wheresoe'er you are' (III.iv.29–37), there is, apart from punctuation and another slight Folio misprint, only one variation, and here it is somewhat doubtful whether the Folio 'pitiless storm' or the Quarto 'pitiless night' is to be preferred. So, in the great speech, 'No, no, no, no! Come, let's away to prison' (V.iii.8–19), there is no difference of wording except that the Quarto omits two of the 'no's' and avoids the Folio's parenthesis-blunder in line 13. The well-rendered speeches are not always Lear's. In the first seventeen lines of Act Fifth, spoken by Edmund and Regan, the Quarto supplies two-and-one-half lines omitted by the Folio, retains a word which the Folio carelessly dropped, and makes two inferior substitutions ('abdication' for 'alteration' and 'I' for 'In'). Otherwise, they are verbally the same.

The passages cited are much above the Quarto's average of correctness, but they are certainly not more untypical than the ones which have been cited to prove its corruptness. It is not likely that Burbage himself could have recited *Lear* from memory with as little error as appears in the better pages of the Quarto text. That such lines could have been so well set down from the recollection of a hireling actor or by any kind of stenography then known exceeds credibility.

If the Quarto is too good to be a reported text, it is too bad to have served as 'copy' for the Folio. Daniel's theory that it was so used does little credit to the good faith of the Folio editors, who on that assumption went out of their way to put one of the 'stolen and surreptitious copies' they were deploring at the base of their purer text. It would be easier to write out clean any average page of *King Lear* than to do the re-lining, re-punctuating, capitalizing, transposing, and substituting of words necessary to make a Quarto page conform to the Folio readings —and the difference to the Folio printer would have been unspeakable. Considering that Heminge and Condell had in their service experts whose business was the making of fair copies, but whose skill in textual collation may well be doubted, it would have been asinine to adopt so cumbrous and dangerous a means of reproducing their theatre manuscript. And why should the editors of the Folio go to the trouble of cutting out the hundreds of undoubtedly Shakespearean lines which only the Quarto prints, while at the same time writing into its pages the lines which it lacks. It would have been a senseless way to proceed, whether considered as a means of giving Shakespeare's works to the world ('cured, and perfect of their limbs,' as they boasted) or as a means of conveniently providing the Folio printer with copy.

It would be a very bigoted editor who would ignore the Quarto text. In the present edition about one hundred and fifty Quarto readings have been accepted as clearly more Shakespearean than their Folio parallels; but, where judgment is difficult between the two texts, the Folio has been preferred, because it is the purer version on the whole and, when it diverges from the original, is more likely to sin in stagy over-heightening than in positive misrepresentation of the poet's meaning. It must be admitted, however, that in some of these cases the preference of the Folio is more the result of prudence and a desire for consistency than of poetic faith. Most of the dubious choices are discussed in the notes.

The Quartos indicate no division of the play into either acts or scenes. The Folio is admirably divided throughout, and is here followed with no change except to translate its Latin 'Actus Primus. Scaena Prima,' *etc.*, to increase the scenes in Act Second from two to four, and regularize the numbering of scenes in Act Fourth. Stage directions are fairly full and accurate in both texts. As usual, those of the Folio show signs of revision by the prompter, and the Quarto wording is here often preferred as more likely to be Shakespeare's. Necessary amplifications and other necessary matter omitted in the original editions are supplied within square brackets ([ ]).

In Shakespeare's usage it was optional to give full syllabic value to the ending *-ed* of past verbal forms or (as is generally done now) to contract this ending with the preceding syllable. In the present edition final *-ed* must always be pronounced as a separate syllable in order to preserve the original rhythm of the verse. Where rhythm requires the contracted form, the spelling *'d* is used.

Shakespeare accented a number of words on syllables which do not now bear the accent, and sometimes his practice in this matter was inconsistent. Where an unusual accentuation is required, it is indicated by an acute mark over the stressed vowel, as in *revénues*.

Obsolete words and words employed in now unusual senses are explained in footnotes the first time they occur in the text. Repetitions are not usually noted and when they occur can be found in the *Index of Words Glossed* at the end of the volume.

The critical and general notes in the following pages are announced by the symbol, *cf. n.*, at the bottom of the page of text to which each has relevance. A name at the end of a note (in parentheses) indicates the authority; but no special effort is made to give credit for material which is common property or which is, so far as known, new in the present edition.

I.i.S.d. *King Lear's Palace.* Shakespeare probably assumed this scene to take place in Leicester, 'Leir-cester,' which, as Holinshed informed him, was built by King Lear and named after him. Leicester is about half way between Liverpool and London in the geographical center of England.

I.i.5–7. *equalities . . . moiety.* The division is so equal as between these two beneficiaries that neither Albany nor Cornwall could find even frivolous reason for preferring the other's share. We are to understand that Lear's plans for dividing his kingdom into three parts are complete and are known to Kent and Gloucester. Only the formal ratifying ceremony remains. The two noblemen are discussing one of the smaller aspects of the abdication; namely, that in arranging it Lear has not allowed his preference of Albany over Cornwall to appear.

I.i.37–55. This speech is a good text for studying the theory that the Quarto version of the play is a 'reconstruction,' based upon an actor's memory, shorthand notes, or both. The Quarto lacks seven lines that are in the Folio and makes four important verbal substitutions: '*first intent*' (39), '*business of our state*' (40), '*Confirming* them on younger *years*' (41), '*Where merit doth most* challenge *it*' (54). It has three metrically short lines, in addition to the last. Otherwise it is a pretty faithful parallel to the Folio, and as a dramatic unit the shortened speech holds together well.

I.i.46. *France and Burgundy*. Both titles would be anachronisms in the prehistoric period in which *Lear* is set. Shakespeare is probably thinking of the fifteenth-century princes thus entitled whom he had dealt with in *Henry V* and *Henry VI*. See R. A. Law, 'Waterish Burgundy,' *Studies in Philology*, 1936, pp. 222–227.

I.i.54. *Where . . . challenge*. Where natural affection competes with the merit of the recipient as chief motive for my gift.

I.i.72. *she names my very deed of love*. The love she talks about is that which I practise in very deed.

I.i.75. *square*. All the joys that manifest themselves through the various senses are thought of as laid out on an area or 'square' of sensibility as on a map. This seems better than to take *square* as a measuring instrument, a carpenter's square.

I.i.79. *More richer*. The Quarto reading. The phrase occurs also in *Hamlet* III.ii.307. The Folio has 'More ponderous.'

I.i.84. Printed as in the Folio. The Quarto has 'Although the last, not least in our dear love.'

I.i.136. *still*. The Quarto word. The Folio has 'shall,' possibly copied from 'shall' in the line above.

I.i.138. *The sway*. These words, attached to line 137 in the Folio and prefixed to line 139 in the Quarto, belong metrically to neither.

I.i.141. *coronet*. Perhaps the award intended for Cordelia as best beloved of his children (W. Perrett).

I.i.151. *Reverse thy doom*. Abrogate your decree. The Quarto reading seems clearly better here than the Folio 'Reserve thy state.' The latter could hardly mean anything but 'keep your pomp,' which in lines 136, 137 Lear has done. The Quarto *stoops* is also preferable to the Folio's 'falls' in this line.

I.i.156. *Reverb no hollowness*. There was a proverb, 'Empty vessels have the loudest sounds,' which Kent is applying to the case of Cordelia and her sisters. (The Quarto reading, 'sound reverbs,' may be the better here.)

I.i.162. *by Apollo*. The play is designedly pre-Christian. By Holinshed's chronology Lear lived in the ninth century B.C., before the founding of Rome. He swears by Apollo and Jupiter (181), or their Celtic equivalents, and, as in lines 110–112, by the sun and stars.

I.i.163. *O vassal! miscreant!* Vague terms of opprobrium. The Quarto reading 'Vassal, recreant' might have the preciser meaning, 'perfidious subject.'

I.i.171. *That.* The formal language of judicial sentence: 'for that,' 'forasmuch as.' It depends on *reward* in line 175. The Quarto has 'Since,' which is easier but more colloquial.

I.i.171. *us.* In changing from *me* (line 170) to *us*, Lear marks his assumption of royal dignity and power.

I.i.175. *Our . . . good.* That is, assuming again and asserting the royal power which I have been talking of relinquishing.

I.i.176. *Five days.* So the Folio. The Quarto, which in general gives rather the better version of this speech, has 'four days,' and in line 178 'fift' instead of *sixt.* There is a similar inconsistency between 'nine' and 'ten' in *Othello* I.iii.279. The explanation may be that Shakespeare used Roman letters for numerals. In Elizabethan script *v* and *x* often had a preliminary stroke which could cause them to be read *iv*, *ix*.

I.i.177. *diseases.* The Quarto word. The Folio 'disasters' seems to be a misprint.

I.i.182. *revok'd.* Ironically echoing Kent's word, line 167.

I.i.187. *your large speeches may your deeds approve.* I hope that your deeds will make good your lavish speeches.

I.i.201. *that little-seeming substance.* Her mere physical presence, small as it seems; *i.e.,* Cordelia without dower.

I.i.221. *folds of favor.* Lear's love has been wrapped around Cordelia like a rich oriental garment, fold over fold.

I.i.224. *which.* Of the two alternatives France has just mentioned, he politicly omits to develop the second (namely, that Lear is at fault) and returns to the first, which reflects on Cordelia. (The Quarto gives the better text of this speech.)

I.i.230. *murther.* The early texts agree in putting this word in Cordelia's mouth and there is no reason for questioning it. The atmosphere of the play is primitive. Cordelia may not unnaturally imagine herself suspected of the crime her sisters so easily commit.

I.i.271. *The jewels.* A vocative: O you who are the jewels.

I.i.282. *well . . . wanted.* Well deserve the loss of the inheritance that you have missed.

I.i.283. *plighted.* The image is the same as in line 221 above. The sisters' real purposes are wrapped in fold on fold of cunning. (In the next line *covers* may be read as a plural, like *stands* in line 242.)

I.i.306. *sit.* That is, in order to continue this conversation. There is nothing to be said in favor of the Quarto reading here, 'hit together.'

I.ii.21. *taw*. It can hardly be doubted that this is what Shakespeare wrote. The word *taw*, originally to tan or curry leather, is well illustrated by a line in Jonson's *Bartholomew Fair* (1614) IV.v.78, 'You know where you were taw'd lately, both lash'd and slash'd you were in Bridewell.' The printers, however, could make nothing of it. Instead of *taw th'*, the Folio has 'to'th'' and the Quarto 'tooth'.' The eighteenth-century emendation, 'top the legitimate,' which makes good but not vivid sense, is commonly adopted. One great objection to this has always been that a final 'p' is a very unlikely letter to be overlooked, either in pronunciation or on the written page.

I.ii.24. *prescrib'd*. The Folio reading, clearly correct. The Quarto has 'subscrib'd.'

I.ii.26. *What news?* In Edmund's letter, of course.

I.ii.43. *too blame*. A common Elizabethan misunderstanding of 'to blame,' *blame* being taken for an adjective (blameworthy).

I.ii.62,63. *thrown . . . closet*. Shakespeare borrows this device from his play of *Julius Caesar* (I.iii.144f., II.i.35), where in turn it is borrowed from Plutarch's life of Caesar.

I.ii.84. *should*. More deferential than 'will' or 'shall.'

I.ii.92,93. *I will . . . this*. Shakespeare makes Edmund repeat the trick Iago had employed in *Othello* IV.i.82ff.

I.ii.100. *wind me into him*. Get into his confidence. The 'ethical dative,' *me*, means 'for my sake.' It was commonly used and often has such light emphasis that it can hardly be paraphrased.

I.ii.106. *These late eclipses*. A topical allusion, connecting the play with the very recent experience of the first spectators. An eclipse of the moon on 27 September 1605 was followed two weeks later (12 October) by an eclipse of the sun.

I.ii.109. *sequent effects*. The next two sentences depict the outburst of suspicion, fear, and brutality that followed the discovery of the Gunpowder Plot, 5 November 1605.

I.ii.114. *falls . . . nature*. Ceases to be governed by the natural instinct (to love one's daughter). A figure from the game of bowls. The 'bias' was the asymmetrical structure of the balls which forced them to roll in a peculiar course.

I.ii.132. *dragon's tail*. Referring to the position of the moon with relation to the long constellation Draco.

I.ii.140. *Fa, sol, la, mi*. This is mere trolling nonsense, based on the notes of the old musical scale.

I.ii.189. *All with me's meet that I can fashion fit.* With me any action is correct which I can make to suit my purpose. In the last six lines Edmund, left alone on the stage, steps out of his character and by a recognized Elizabethan convention speaks objectively and informatively to the audience.

I.iii.S.d. *Duke of Albany's Palace.* Albany was the old name of North Britain, above the Humber River. York, a very ancient city which was the military capital of Roman Britain, would be the natural residence of Goneril and her husband. It is a hundred miles north of Leicester.

I.iii.21. *With . . . abus'd.* The line, found only in the Quarto text, is most likely incorrect. A sense can be given to it by taking *as* to mean 'as well as' and *abus'd* 'misguided.'

I.iv.1. *If but as well, etc.* That is, if I can disguise my voice as well as I have changed my looks.

I.iv.18. *fish.* Possibly an anachronistic jest meaning 'I am ultra-Protestant,' keyed to the strong anti-Catholic feeling aroused by the Gunpowder Plot.

I.iv.19. *What art thou?* Lear repeats the question Kent has twice humorously evaded (lines 9, 12). Kent evades again.

I.iv.40. *forty-eight.* It has been suggested that Kent's part was specially written to fit John Heminge, one of the 'sharers' in Shakespeare's company and later the senior editor of the Folio. The age of Kent is not suggested by any of the sources and it would fit with Heminge's at the time the play was produced. See T. S. Baldwin, *Organization and Personnel of the Shakespearean Company,* p. 250.

I.iv.68. *remember'st . . . conception.* You remind me of what I have myself thought.

I.iv.87. *football.* Football was a rough game for rough village lads, not regarded as a gentleman's sport. It was in special (but not exclusive) vogue in the North (see note on II.ii.85).

I.iv.100,101. The Quarto is here correct. The Folio accidentally substitutes Lear's speech in line 110.

I.iv.116. *the Lady-brach.* This, one fears, alludes to Goneril. The Quarto has 'Ladie oth'e brach.'

I.iv.118. *A pestilent gall to me.* The Fool's talk rubs me shrewdly where I am sore. Lear, however, whose conscience has begun to hurt him, is not ungrateful for this counter-irritant and encourages it for the distraction it affords.

I.iv.122–126. *Have . . . trowest.* These precepts of worldly wisdom may be paraphrased: Don't display all you have, don't tell all you know, don't lend all you own, don't disregard your own comfort, don't believe all you are told.

I.iv.130,131. *thou shalt have more Than two tens to a score.* If you do all this, you will have more than maximum felicity.

I.iv.147. *Do thou for him stand.* A masterpiece of indirect arraignment. The king can do no wrong, but the king can stand for the hypothetical lord who counselled the king to the king's own folly.

I.iv.157. *monopoly out.* This alludes to a common commercial abuse in Shakespeare's time. Individuals or companies were granted the exclusive right to trade in various commodities (as wine, sugar, *etc.*), and often thus amassed huge fortunes. The sense of *out* is 'issued in my name.'

I.iv.168,169. *let . . . so.* Any one who condemns the Fool's reasoning about Lear's distribution of the kingdom must be a knave and deserves whipping.

I.iv.172. *wits to wear.* Behind this nonsense verse, and in other parts of the play, one detects a scornful protest against the new foppery and social extravagance that James I's accession brought in.

I.iv.181. *play bo-peep.* Erratically display and conceal his royal countenance, as a nurse does her face to amuse an infant. This stanza is a parody of a popular pious ballad written by John Careless, one of the martyrs of Queen Mary's time (for text, see H. E. Rollins, *Old English Ballads*, 1920, pp. 47ff.).

I.iv.203. *Weary of all, shall want some.* Tired of possessing everything, shall find himself lacking even the portion that he needs. The story of Lear in a nutshell.

I.iv.222. *it.* An old possessive case, of which Shakespeare seems to have been fond as a relief from the neuter *his*, especially in childish talk.

I.iv.230. *Whoop . . . thee. Jug* was a pet-name for Joan, and the words may be quoted from a current song. They are inspired by Goneril's speech just above, on which the Fool comments: any ass can tell when the cart is drawing the horse; *i.e.*, when the relation of father and child is unnaturally inverted. And then, with sardonic reference to Goneril, he trolls: 'Whoop! how I do love you!'

I.iv.240. *Which they.* The antecedent is not clear. Lear's speech above, badly preserved in the Quarto which alone contains it, was evidently in verse. Only the last line of it now scans.

I.iv.267. *sea-monster.* The dreadful mythological creature who came for

> The virgin tribute paid by howling Troy
> To the sea-monster (*Merchant of Venice* III.ii.56).

I.iv.298,299. *that scope As.* Such scope as, whatever scope. The Quarto has the easier 'that scope that.'

I.iv.300. *fifty of my followers at a clap.* The two texts agree in this puzzling line. One might suspect that Lear has discovered, in the brief moment he has been off the stage, that Goneril has somehow liquidated fifty knights, though she has threatened nothing so drastic. However, in the next act (II.iv.205–208) Lear still has his hundred knights, as he has on Goneril's word in line 339 below. It looks as if some change was made in the play at this point. See E. S. Noyes, 'On the Dismissal of Lear's Knights and Goneril's Letter to Regan,' *Philological Quarterly*, 1930, pp. 297–303.

I.iv.324–328. The main virtuosity about this piece of doggerel appears to be that the Fool sings it in rustic dialect, making all the final words rime: ca't her, da'ter, sla'ter, ha'ter, a'ter.

I.iv.350. *atask'd.* For the elaborate bibliographical structure which has been built upon this word, see W. W. Greg, *The Editorial Problem in Shakespeare*, 1942, p. 98. The printer of the Quarto first set up 'alapt,' which can hardly be anything but a misreading of 'ataxt.' The error was discovered while the Quarto was being printed and in certain copies 'attaskt' was substituted. The Folio printed 'at task.' 'Tax' and 'task' (the same word originally) were both commonly used in the sense of 'blame.' Shakespeare might have used whichever he liked (and on other occasions employed both with this meaning), but (perhaps only for the sake of rhythm) he preferred to invent a derived form, either 'atax' or 'atask,' which apparently no one else has ever used. The new word seems to have reached the Quarto printer in the form 'ataxt' and the Folio printer in the form 'attaskt' and in each case it made trouble; but it is doubtful whether more can be read into the situation than the presumption that the two texts were set up from different manuscripts.

I.v.1. *Gloucester.* The residence of Regan and Cornwall and capital of the southwestern section of Lear's kingdom. A very ancient city, important in Roman and Anglo-Saxon times, about seventy-five miles southwest of Leicester.

I.v.12. *Thy wit shall not go slipshod.* One of the Fool's poorer and more acid jokes. If men's brains were liable to chilblains like their heels, you would be immune, because you have so little brain. He is desperately attempting to prevent Lear from brooding.

I.v.49.S.d. *The Folio* marks the Gentleman's entrance (erroneously) with the rest at the opening of the scene. This is the textual convention known as 'massed entrances.'

I.v.53,54. *departure . . . shorter.* Pronounced in vulgar fashion, 'departer . . . sharter.' This parting obscenity is addressed to the audience after Lear has gone out. (The Fool, it should be remembered, is an adolescent boy.)

II.i.S.d. *Castle.* This is on a treeless and uncultivated heath, a day's ride from the city of Gloucester. Shakespeare was doubtless thinking of one of the British Camps, the remains of which are conspicuous on the crests of hills (*e.g.*, the one near Dorchester on the Thames which he would have passed in going from Stratford to London). Gloucester's castle may appropriately be located in the Vale of the White Horse or Salisbury Plain or, perhaps more plausibly, in one of the bleaker parts of the Cotswolds, *e.g.*, near Chipping Norton.

II.i.1. *Curan.* A name not found in any of the sources. It is probably suggested by the popular story of Curan and Argentile in William Watson's *Albion's England,* first printed in 1586. Curan seems to be a confidential agent of Gloucester who finds it worth his while to pass on to Edmund the information that he picks up.

II.i.19. *Briefness and fortune, work!* Let me leave it to quick action and luck.

II.i.40,41. *Mumbling . . . mistress.* A clear effort at pagan atmosphere.

II.i.46. *But that.* That is, he could by no means so persuade me but that (in spite of what he said) I told him.

II.i.53. *latch'd.* Shakespeare is fond of this word and probably used it here, as the Folio records. The Quarto has 'lancht,' *i.e.*, lanced, a more obvious verb.

II.i.59. *found—dispatch.* When he is found, a quick death to him!

II.i.63. *caitiff.* The Quarto word, more expressive than 'Coward,' which the Folio substitutes.

II.i.93. *He whom my father nam'd.* This tells us by Elizabethan convention that Lear's name was also Edgar; but the reference to 'godson' and the Anglo-Saxon name are both anachronisms.

II.i.101. *expense and waste.* Folio reading. The Quarto text is an interesting illustration of publishers' methods. The printer set up 'these—and wast,' the first part of which (which perhaps should have been printed 'the—se') seems to be an honest confession of failure to make anything of the indecipherable combination 'thexpense.' The Quarto corrector, out of his own head, changed this to 'the wast and spoyle,' which appears in some of the copies.

II.i.113. *How . . . please.* Employing my power as you will.

II.i.121. *poise.* The Folio prints 'prize' and the Quarto printer first set up 'prise,' but this was corrected in certain copies of the Quarto to 'poyse.'

II.i.126. *From . . . dispatch.* Are waiting to be started on their way from there.

II.ii.S.d. Kent and Oswald have both ridden all night. Kent, having arrived a little earlier, is taken by Oswald for a native of the place.

II.ii.7. *I love thee not.* The particular reason for Kent's rage against Oswald appears in scene fourth of this act, lines 27ff.

II.ii.9. *Lipsbury pinfold.* Lipsbury, a place unknown to geographical research, must be a Shakespearean coinage, and can hardly mean anything but 'Lip-Town.' A pinfold is a village pound in which straying beasts are corraled. 'Lipsbury pinfold,' then, is where one may expect 'lippy' creatures like Oswald, with vagrant tongues and habits, to wind up. Kent says If I had you in an appropriate place from which you couldn't escape, I would make you care for me. Both the texts print the phrase with perfect correctness, though the printers can hardly have known what it meant.

II.ii.16. *three-suited.* This has been sometimes taken to indicate poverty of wardrobe, but *cf.* III.iv.133, *who hath had three suits to his back,* where Edgar plainly alludes to a former state of affluence. It may refer to a servant's liveries, and thus would be a natural term of contempt applied to Oswald; and Edgar, in the later passage, would refer to the 'enough and to spare' enjoyed by hired servants. At the extortionate price of Elizabethan clothes the possession of three suits was quite beyond the ordinary man. Similarly *hundred-pound* and *worsted-stocking* suggest luxury. Kent is contrasting the pampered lackey's outward exquisiteness with his mental and moral poverty.

II.ii.33. *sop o' th' moonshine.* A sop was bread soaked in wine or other liquid. Kent will make Oswald's body so porous with holes that it will suck up the moonbeams he has just mentioned.

II.ii.47. *With you.* Let me have a word (and a blow) with you.

Kent continues to address Oswald, refusing to be diverted by Edmund.

I.ii.66. *zed.* The current name of the letter 'z.' It had an ornate orthographic form, was seldom used (because its work was generally done by 's'), and so is an image of the social parasite.

I.ii.77,78. *holy cords . . . too intrinse.* The holy cords are the bonds of affection between father and daughters. The idea is repeated in Cleopatra's lines to the asp, *Antony and Cleopatra* V.ii.306f.:

> With thy sharp teeth this knot intrinsicate
> Of life at once untie.

I.ii.81. *halcyon.* The kingfisher. The popular superstition was that, if a dead kingfisher were hung up, his bill would point toward the quarter from which the wind was blowing.

I.ii.85. *Smoil.* Both the texts read *Smoile* ('smoyle'), a Northern dialect form of 'smile,' meaning presumably 'smile at.' It is used in Tennyson's *Northern Farmer (Old Style)*, line 53. It looks as if Oswald was represented on the stage as a somewhat farcical Yorkshireman (*cf.* I.iv.86,87), and Kent seems to be parodying his accent.

I.ii.87. *Camelot.* Supposed to have been in Somerset (or Cornwall), but the Elizabethans identified it with Winchester and believed that King Arthur's round table was still to be seen there (see the play of *Eastward Hoe* V.i., composed about a year before *King Lear*). Winchester is about a day's journey by foot from Sarum (Salisbury) Plain. The *goose . . . Camelot* collocation contains an allusion to the unsavory disease known to Shakespeare as 'Winchester goose.' The idea is the same as in lines 9, 10 above.

I.ii.97. *better faces.* Kent's opinion of Cornwall is hinted at in the first lines of the play.

I.ii.112. *Flickering on.* Quarto: 'In flitkering.' Folio: 'On flicking.' 'Flickering' in this sense was perhaps original with Shakespeare; it puzzled the compositors.

I.ii.117. *your displeasure.* 'your Displeasure,' an ironic honorific, modelled on 'your Excellence,' 'your Grace,' *etc.*

I.ii.129. *Ajax.* According to their own account, Ajax is but a ninny beside them. In *Love's Labor's Lost* V.ii.578, Ajax is runner-up for a place among the Nine Worthies.

I.ii.136. *Stocking.* As a royal messenger, Kent had the immunity of heralds, and the stocks were punishment for low misdemeanors and vulgar malefactors.

II.ii.147. *vilest and contemned'st.* The reading is uncertain. The Quarto, which alone contains the line, originally had 'beles and contaned' which in some copies was changed to 'basest and temnest.' (See Greg, *Variants*, p. 54.)

II.ii.150,151. *That . . . restrain'd.* Here, except that the Folio has 'he' instead of *he's*, the two texts agree in a reading which does not make sense. Perhaps a line dropped out after 150.

II.ii.165. *heaven's benediction.* The proverb, with 'God's blessing' instead of *heaven's benediction,* is, as Kent says, common; but the instances that have been found do not explain what God's blessing is. Probably, the beneficent rain; and probably the saw was meant to rebuke those who forsake a dull and salutary way of life in search of something more garish. The mention of 'the warm sun' in line 166 motivates Kent's following address to the luminary, which is now about to rise. The whole scene has taken place in the obscure light of dawn.

II.ii.169,170. *Nothing . . . misery.* This, by admitting, palliates the improbability that Kent should at this time have an unread letter from Cordelia. Shakespeare is fond of the trick. The words mean: The strangest good fortune comes when one is most miserable.

II.ii.173–175. *And . . . remedies.* The last words of Cordelia's letter, offering hope that she may be able to remedy Lear's losses. 'This enormous state' may mean no more than the weighty business of the French crown.

II.iii. In the Folio, Scene Second continues to the end of the act. What modern editors mark as Scene Third has no local designation. It registers the passage of several hours, while Kent sleeps. Edgar simply appears on the front stage, without particular indication of where he is, makes his soliloquy to the audience, and goes out, after which the action of Scene Second resumes in what we call Scene Fourth.

II.iii.14. *Bedlam beggars.* Former inmates of Bedlam (Bethlehem Hospital for the insane) in London, who had been discharged as partially cured, and licensed to solicit charity. This is a contemporary (seventeenth-century) touch.

II.iii.20. *Turlygod . . . Tom.* The Bedlamites solicited their alms under the name of 'Poor Tom' or 'Tom o' Bedlam.' *Turlygod* is spelled in just this way in both the original texts, capitalized and italicized as a proper name. The Quarto, having first printed 'Tuelygod,' is at pains to correct the 'e' to 'r' on the revised forme. Yet the name has not been found elsewhere. It may be a form of 'twirligig' (whirligig). A word 'grinagod' (also 'grinagog') means one who is always grinning, on the analogy of which 'turligod' would be one always whirling or being whirled about, the sport of chance (O. E. D.).

II.iv.24. *To do upon respect such violent outrage.* To outrage decency so violently.

II.iv.38–42. *And . . . drew.* Kent is too angry to be coherent. And I, he means, meeting the other messenger, drew my sword.

II.iv.56,57. *mother . . . Hysterica passio.* These terms are taken from Harsnet's pamphlet on witchcraft and demoniacal possession, which suggested so much of Edgar's mad talk. See note on III.iv.53. Both the early texts of the play, naturally enough, read 'Historica,' corrected in the fourth Folio of 1685.

II.iv.76. *none but knaves.* The Fool does not accept the opportunist doctrine he has just cynically stated.

II.iv.102,104. Text as in Quarto (corrected forme).

II.iv.140. *scant.* So the Folio. The Quarto has 'slack,' and Shakespeare doubtless wrote one or the other, though strict logic would require a word with the opposite meaning such as 'perform.'

II.iv.147,148. *on . . . confine.* A very fine figure. Lear's powers (like the owner of an estate) have travelled over all the territory that is theirs and now stand on the extreme edge, viewing that over which they have no control.

II.iv.159. *She . . . train.* See note on I.iv.300 and lines 205–208 below.

II.iv.172. *tender-hefted.* Responsive to the hilt, easily managed. A figure from a knife or other instrument in which the haft or handle easily accommodates itself to the master's use. The term can perhaps be illustrated by Osric's talk about rapiers in *Hamlet* V.ii.152ff.

II.iv.224. *bile.* So spelled in the early editions ('byle,' 'bile') and so commonly pronounced.

II.iv.235. *mingle . . . passion.* Do not receive your wild words at face value, but discount them in the light of reason. The figure, however, is that of mixing a drink.

II.iv.268–271. *Thou . . . warm.* Lear here becomes very modern and proves his point by reference to the costume of a lady of fashion at James I's court. If we assume, he says, that the purpose of gorgeous raiment is to keep the wearer warm, then (1) nature does not need such extravagance of dress, and (2) this dress, cut according to the fashion of the day, hardly keeps the wearer warm anyway.

II.iv.294–296. *So am I . . . return'd.* These speeches are differently assigned in the Quarto, the first to Cornwall and the second to Regan. The Quarto likewise gives Cornwall's speech line 299, to Regan.

II.iv.301. *bleak.* The Quarto word. Folio, 'high.'

II.iv.310. *storm.* The storm, which plays so large a rôle in *Ac Third*, had no place in the Lear story before Shakespeare. He took it, along with the tale of Gloucester and his sons, from Sidney's *Arcadia* (ed. 1590, Bk.ii, ch. 10). See Appendix A

III.i.10. *little world of man.* Lear, whose rage is in unison with that of the storm, illustrates the metaphysical doctrine that the 'microcosm,' man, lives in a complex harmony with the 'macrocosm' or universe or world of 'things' (see line 7).

III.i.29. *furnishings.* The sentence is incomplete, and, since Quarto cut here immediately precedes a Folio cut, it is possible that an intermediate line or two may have been omitted by both texts (Greg), but nothing important for the sense seems to have been lost.

III.ii.23. *high-engender'd battles.* Battalions of rain and wind produced high in the air.

III.ii.30. *So beggars marry many.* So many beggars marry; *i.e.* before they have a roof over their heads.

III.ii.31,32. The *toe* stands for Goneril and Regan, the *heart* for Cordelia. He who misplaces his affection upon that which is meanest.

III.ii.71. *vile.* This word is regularly spelled 'vild' or 'vilde' in both the early texts.

III.ii.76. *Must make content with his fortunes fit.* Must fit contentment to his fortunes, be satisfied with what he has.

III.ii.79–96. Comic relief, which at this point is badly needed. It would be unreasonable to suppose that Shakespeare did not write it. It is a parody of the famous prophecy of Merlin, of which one text was printed in Elizabethan texts of Chaucer and in Puttenham's *Art of English Poetry*, 1589, whence Shakespeare may have got it. The first four lines describe conditions current in Shakespeare's England; the next six describe absurdly utopian conditions; and the conclusion (lines 91,92) is that when these things come together, the realm of Albion will be in great confusion.

III.ii.83. *nobles are their tailors' tutors.* Noblemen spend their time teaching their tailors new fashions.

III.ii.84. *No . . . suitors.* No heretics except lying lovers; no burnings except from venereal disease.

III.ii.86. *nor no poor knight.* And no knight poor.

II.ii.93,94. *Then . . . feet.* After the imposing build-up, the prophecy ends, as such things often did, in a flat truism: When people walk, they will do it with their feet.

II.ii.95. *Merlin.* A playful anachronism. Merlin was the magician of King Arthur's court. By the chronology Shakespeare followed, the Fool would have lived about 1300 years before his time.

II.iv.17-19. *In such a night . . . In such a night as this!* Consciously antiphonal, it would seem, to the joyous duet of Lorenzo and Jessica: 'in such a night as this . . . in such a night' (*Merchant of Venice* V.i).

II.iv.20. *Your one kind father, whose frank heart gave you all.* Here the Quarto text is better. The Folio, by omitting *you*, gets the conventional count of syllables, but puts the accent on the wrong words. Stress *fath'r, frank,* and *gave*.

II.iv.36. *shake the superflux.* The figure is from shaking the branches of an over-laden fruit tree.

II.iv.53. *halters in his pew.* The word *pew* is for the sake of grisly impropriety and to show how ubiquitous the fiend's temptation is. He lays knives under his pillow when he sleeps, puts hangman's nooses in his pew when he prays, sets ratsbane by his porridge when he eats. Lewis Theobald (1688-1744) was the first to show that the allusions to superstitions and fiends in Edgar's simulated ravings were largely taken from Samuel Harsnet's *Declaration of Egregious Popish Impostures,* 1603. Harsnet tells of a man who brought home a new halter and two knives; whereupon the devil 'laid them in the gallery, that some of those that were possessed might either hang themselves with the halter or kill themselves with the blades.' This is doubtless Shakespeare's source, though similar passages are found in Marlowe's *Doctor Faustus* (lines 632ff.) and Spenser's *Faery Queen* (Bk.I, canto ix, st. 22ff.)

II.iv.60. *There . . . now.* He picks at different parts of his body, as if the foul fiend were vexing him in the bites of vermin.

II.iv.74. *pelican.* In the natural history of the time the young pelican is the type of ungrateful progeny, because fostered on its parents' blood.

II.iv.75. *Pillicock.* 'Pelican' suggests to Edgar this vulgar word, which he fancifully distorts into a bird of prey sitting on its hill.

II.iv.98,99. *Hay . . . sessa.* Essentially as in Quarto. The Folio expands strangely: 'Sayes, suum, mun, nonny, Dolphin my

Boy, Boy *Sesey*.' The last word, spelled 'caese' in Quarto, is probably the same exclamation which occurs in III.vi.73, where the Folio spells it 'sese,' and in IV.vi.199.

III.iv.138. *Smulkin*. Smulkin, like Modo and Mahu mentioned below (line 142), was among the devils exorcised in the witch findings discussed in Harsnet's book (see note on line 53 above).

III.iv.164–168. *I had a son, etc.* Edgar, who has been using mad talk as a shield against recognition, becomes almost speechless on hearing this disclosure.

III.iv.179–181. The first line may be from some lost romance; the last two are from the popular ballad of *Jack the Giant killer*. They are Edgar's mystical way of saying that he sees a dark adventure before him and smells a rat.

III.iv.181. *British man*. 'English man' in the ballad, but there were no Englishmen in Lear's time, and when Shakespeare was writing this play there was a new movement to call all inhabitants of the island 'British' in recognition of the union with Scotland. James I had been proclaimed King of Great Britain, 24 October 1604.

III.vi.4. *have*. The preceding word, *wits*, has caused the verb to take the plural form. Shakespeare was capable of this and both the texts have it so, but it may be a scribal error.

III.vi.5.S.d. *Enter Lear, etc.* The Quarto has these characters enter with Kent and Gloucester at the opening of the scene, but the Folio arrangement is evidently correct. Edgar has been holding back to avoid recognition by his father. Lear has kept with Edgar, and the Fool with Lear.

III.vi.6. *Frateretto*. Listed by Harsnet with Flibbertigibbet (*cf.* III.iv.113) in his group of devils. The following allusion to Nero may be a vague recollection of Rabelais (bk. ii.30).

III.vi.25. *broom*. In the old song the word is 'bourn,' brook; but Edgar may be intentionally misquoting, with a hint at witches and broomsticks.

III.vi.41–44. *Sleepest . . . harm.* Based on some version of the nursery rime of 'Little Boy Blue,' as lines 25–28 are based on another popular song. In Edgar's perversion line 43 probably means 'If you give me one kiss.'

III.vi.45. *Purr! the cat is grey.* Hinting that it is an old grey witch who is wheedling the jolly shepherd. Lear seizes the suggestion and identifies her with Goneril.

III.vi.46–48. *'Tis Goneril . . . father.* So the first Quarto. The second Quarto (perhaps rightly) adds 'she' before *kicked*.

II.vi.51. *joint-stool.* A joint-stool was one made by joiners, as opposed to the usual rough home-made ones. The frequent mention of this article illustrates the scarcity of good furniture in Shakespeare's time. Lear, of course, in his delirium identifies the stool with Goneril.

II.vi.68. *brach or him.* So the early texts. Instead of *him* Sir Thomas Hanmer (1677–1746) conjectured 'lym' in the sense of 'lyme-hound,' bloodhound; but that use is not well supported, and a misreading of manuscript 'l' as 'h' is not likely.

II.vi.80. *Persian.* The customary epithet for gorgeous attire from the days of the Greeks and Romans. At the time *Lear* was written the travels of the Sherley brothers had called attention to the opportunities of trade with Persia.

II.vi.83. *We'll go to supper i' th' morning.* Lear is hungry, but his weariness exceeds his hunger, and by royal decree (*We'll go*) he postpones supper till the morning.

II.vi.85. *And I'll go to bed at noon.* Fool's logic. If supper takes place in the morning, bedtime will come at noon. The words are the last the Fool speaks and they hint a sort of author's apology for closing his career in the middle of the play. If the Fool's part was written for Robert Armin, as many think, there seems less reason for the otherwise plausible theory that the Fool's sudden disappearance and the scantiness of Cordelia's part are both due to the need Shakespeare found to give the two rôles to a single boy actor. On the other hand, if Armin played only the Fool, it seems strange that so conspicuous an actor should have been allowed no appearance in the fourth or fifth act. The likelihood is that Armin, who was not very old, was obliged to undertake the part of Cordelia as well as his normal one, for Goneril and Regan made big demands on the available boys in the company. (It may be too venturous to suggest that these famous words, found only in the Folio, may have been added by Armin himself rather than Shakespeare.)

I.vi.117. *Lurk, lurk!* In the Quarto version (which alone contains this speech) Edgar conceals himself as Cornwall *et al.* enter the stage for Scene Seventh.

I.vii.42. *simple-answer'd.* Straightforward in your reply. The Quarto reads 'simple answerer.'

I.vii.57. *rash.* Here the Folio, which substitutes 'stick,' seems to be sophisticating. *Rash* was a good old verb, used by Malory of the attack of boars, but was becoming rare in standard English in Shakespeare's time. In printing 'rain' for *rage* in line

61 and 'stern' for *dern* in line 62, the Folio seems again to be
preferring the less Shakespearean word.

III.vii.58. *bow'd.* This is a new emendation, but it seems to account for both the Quarto reading 'lou'd' (corrected in some
copies to 'lowd') and the Folio 'bare.' A tragi-grotesque quibble
with *buoy'd* in the next line is probably intentional.

III.vii.60. *stelled fires.* There is a pun in *stelled*, which suggests
both 'stelled,' fixed, and 'stellate,' starry. The shortness of line
60 and the number of hard textual problems both indicate
that this speech of Gloucester's puzzled the printers.

III.vii.64. *All cruels else subscribe.* The Folio reading. The
Quarto has 'subscrib'd.' The clause is concessive and general:
Give sanction and formal allowance, if you like, to all other
cruel creatures, yet I shall see, *etc.*

III.vii.71. *Hold your hand, etc.* The intervention of the servant
in a vain attempt to prevent his master's crime is not in Sidney's *Arcadia*, upon which this portion of the play is based.
It is taken from an actual incident dramatized in the pseudo-
Shakespearean play, *A Yorkshire Tragedy*, produced by Shakespeare's company in the late summer or autumn of 1605, and
therefore throws light upon the date of composition of *King
Lear.* See *Modern Language Notes*, xxvii (1912), p. 62.

IV.i.6. *The . . . laughter.* The familiar image of Fortune's
wheel, constantly revolving. Those on its bottom live in the
element of tears, those on the top in the element of laughter.

IV.i.10. *poorly led.* So the Folio. Edgar has not yet noticed his
father's blindness. The original Quarto reading, 'poorlie, leed'
is probably a misreading of 'poorlie-ledd' and the Quarto corrector's 'parti, eyd' a mere guess.

IV.i.11,12. *But that . . . age.* Only the strange reversals of
worldly fortune make men grow old. The doctrine is similar
to that of Matthew Arnold in *The Scholar Gipsy*, stanzas
17–23.

IV.i.20,21. *Means . . . commodities.* Our resources (or capa-
bilities) make us foolhardy and our bald deficiencies prove to
be advantages.

IV.i.67–71. These lines repeat the social philosophy of III.iv.34–
37.

IV.i.68. *That slaves your ordinance.* Who tramples underfoot
your command (to love one's neighbor as oneself).

IV.i.74. *in the confined deep.* A poetical paraphrase for what
the Elizabethans called 'the narrow seas,' the Strait of Dover.
(*In* means 'into' or 'down upon.')

IV.ii.1. *Welcome, my lord!* Goneril and Edmund have, of course, made the long journey from Gloucester's castle to York (?) together. As they approach her palace, she bids him welcome there.

IV.ii.3. *never man so chang'd.* One of the most successful minor touches in the play is the development in Albany, who is evidently young and honest, and at the opening stands in confused awe of his majestic wife. Goneril's misjudgment of him is a large factor in her downfall.

IV.ii.17. *names.* The Folio reading. If the Quarto 'arms' is correct, the sense is: I must exchange the distaff for the sword.

IV.ii.21. *mistress's.* There is a quibble on two meanings. Ere long I shall challenge you both as queen and lover. She is doubtless planning to detach Edmund from Cornwall's service to her own.

IV.ii.28. *My . . . body.* To be taken with the preceding line. A woman might justly adore Edmund, but Albany in the rôle of husband is as if the foot presumed to control the whole body. This is the reading of the uncorrected Quarto and is doubtless as Shakespeare wrote it, but it was not understood. The Quarto corrector clarified it vulgarly into 'A fool usurps my bed' and the Folio into 'My fool usurps my body.'

IV.ii.29. *worth the whistling.* Alluding to the proverb, 'It is a poor dog that is not worth the whistling'; that is, there was a time when you thought me worthy of attention.

IV.ii.32. *it.* The purpose of the Quarto corrector in changing *it* to 'ith' is obscure. He can hardly have meant to substitute 'its,' for in 1608 that form was very new and rare. Doubtless he did not understand the passage and took this for another of the *i' th'* abbreviations of 'in the.'

IV.ii.39. *Filths savor but themselves.* To the filthy all things are filthy. Suggested by the Latin proverbs, 'puris omnia pura' and 'pravis omnia prava.'

IV.ii.51. *a head for wrongs.* That is, born to be made a cuckold.

IV.ii.52,53. *discerning . . . suffering.* Capable of distinguishing between an advantage and an injury.

IV.ii.54,55. *Fools . . . mischief.* This is greatly condensed. 'Grant that we are all villains,' Goneril seems to mean; 'yet you are involved with the rest of us, and only fools pity the sort of villain you are, who will allow yourself to be punished for treason before you have done any overt act.'

IV.ii.57. *state . . . threat.* Where, as here, the Folio offers no text for comparison, the true reading of this difficult poetry is often obscure. The Quarto compositor read this as 'thy slayer begins threats,' which in certain copies was altered to 'thy state begins thereat.' The emendation is by Charles Jennens (1700–1773).

IV.ii.68. *Mew!* The 'cat-call' employed by an Elizabethan audience to hiss a bad actor.

IV.iii. This sentimental and undramatic scene is certainly Shakespeare's. Its purpose is to reawaken the audience's sympathy for Cordelia, who has been so long absent from the stage and is now about to appear again. The scene is wholly omitted in the Folio, which, of course, throws out the Folio numbering of the remaining scenes in the act (but see note on Scene Seventh). The Quarto printer made, as usual, several blunders, which previous editors have not been very resourceful in clearing up.

IV.iii.12. *Ay, sir.* Quarto 'I say' (explained by Theobald).

IV.iii.30. *believe't.* Quarto 'be beleeft.' (The repetition of 'be' is probably accidental.)

IV.iii.32. *clamor-moisten'd hair.* Quarto 'clamour moystened her.' In Shakespeare ladies' tresses suffer remarkably when they weep. Compare *King John* III.iv.61ff.:

> Bind up those tresses. O what love I note
> In the fair multitude of those her hairs!
> Where but by chance a silver drop hath fallen,
> Even to that drop ten thousand wiry friends
> Do glue themselves in sociable grief.

IV.iii.40. *sometime . . . tune.* Occasionally, when better in tune, *i.e.*, more rational.

IV.v.S.d. *Regan's Palace.* For the presumable place see note on I.v.1. There is no reason to suppose that Regan would continue to live in Gloucester's castle (which she complained of as 'little,' II.iv.289). When she speaks of Goneril's 'late being *here*' in line 24, she means 'in this part of the country,' in the South; or else it is a dramatic license which in Shakespeare's theatre would never be detected.

IV.v.21. *Some things.* Perhaps she begins to say that some things are not to be trusted even to Oswald's discretion, but she checks herself.

IV.v.22. *I had rather––.* Without being disrespectful, Oswald makes it clear that he is incorruptible, and Regan drops her plea to see the letter.

IV.vi.22. *pebble.* So in both texts. A collective plural like 'sand.' 'Pebbles' would be cacophonous here.

IV.vi.24. *deficient sight*. A bold use of metonymy. The dizzy man's failing eyesight is put for the man himself.

IV.vi.34,35. *Why . . . cure it*. The grammar is curiously twisted, but apparently genuine. The two texts agree.

IV.vi.40. *snuff*. The partly consumed wick of a candle, giving smoke rather than light.

IV.vi.42. *Gone, sir: farewell*. The Quarto prints these words following the stage direction (omitted in the Folio) which they here precede. Since they give Gloucester assurance that his instructions in lines 31,32 have been obeyed, they clearly should be spoken before he leaps.

IV.vi.43–45. *conceit . . . theft*. Mere imagination (conceit) may cause death when there is no will to live.

IV.vi.58. *summit*. A rather rare word in the seventeenth century, often spelled 'sommet' as in French. Shakespeare employs it only here and in two passages of *Hamlet* (I.iv.70, III.iii.18), and the earliest texts generally print it 'Somnet,' as in the Folio here. The *Lear* Quarto misrepresents it as 'sommons' and the Folio in the earlier *Hamlet* passage as 'Sonnet.'

IV.vi.73. *fiend*. Edgar's purpose is to give Gloucester a sense of the value of his life by persuading him that the evil powers have attempted to destroy him and the good have preserved him.

IV.vi.87. *Nature's above art*. To be taken with Lear's previous speech. A king cannot be arrested for issuing false currency, for the currency is all the king's and bears his image. Therefore nature (royal birth) is better than the counterfeiter's art. Lear then imagines himself in various occupations of his past life: enlisting soldiers, drilling recruits, indulging in the pastime of ratting, challenging an opponent, calling up the reserves in battle, and attending an archery contest. Finally, he sees Edgar and imagines himself a sentinel on duty.

IV.vi.89. *crow-keeper*. Crow-herd, a boy or old man employed to keep crows off planted fields (and equipped with a makeshift bow).

IV.vi.94. *Sweet marjoram*. Described in Nicholas Culpeper's *Complete Herbal* as 'an excellent remedy for the brain' (E. Blunden, *Shakespeare's Significances*, 1929).

IV.vi.100,101. *'Ay' . . . divinity*. Alluding to St. Paul's words to the Corinthians (2 Cor. I. 18, 19): 'But as God is true, our word toward you was not yea and nay. For the Son of God, Jesus Christ . . . was not yea and nay, but in him was yea.'

IV.vi.110–127. After a line and a half of blank verse matching Gloucester's, Lear reverts to undoubted prose. The Folio made a halfhearted attempt to divide it as poetry and modern editors have gone further, with sad results. It is part of the great irony of the play that this mad barbarian king here interrupts his madness to arraign Jacobean court life.

IV.vi.117. *Whose face between her forks presages snow.* To understand this now it is necessary to read *between her forks* after *snow*.

IV.vi.121. *centaurs.* Hybrids of beast and man. Ben Jonson had the same idea, if not this line, in mind when he called one of the ladies in *The Silent Woman* (1609) Madam Centaur.

IV.vi.131. *Do you.* Quarto reading. The Folio has 'Do'st thou,' but there seems no reason for Gloucester to speak familiarly to his king at this point.

IV.vi.134. *challenge.* The challenge is addressed to Cupid. Compare the opening of *Much Ado about Nothing* (I.i.40), where Beatrice says that Benedick 'challenged Cupid at the flight; and my uncle's fool, reading the challenge, subscribed for Cupid, and challenged him at the bird-bolt.'

IV.vi.149. *handy-dandy.* An expression from a child's game, meaning 'which hand will you have?'—*i.e.*, they both look alike.

IV.vi.155. *in office.* That is, when he has a position of authority. The Quarto has the interesting misprint, 'a dogge, so bade in office,' which is stressed by some critics as evidence that that text depends on hearing rather than the written word. All it means is that the Quarto compositor was here working automatically without his mind on his work and unthinkingly set up the first words suggested by the sounds he was carrying in his head. A subconscious association with 'a dog so bayed' may have put him off the track. The wonder is that the style of *Lear* did not oftener derail him.

IV.vi.158. *lusts.* Second person singular, like *whipp'st* below. Shakespeare was not obliged by current usage to employ the -st form, and did not when it was too cacophonous. (Quarto reading: 'thy bloud hotly lusts.')

IV.vi.160. *Through totter'd rags small vices do appear.* Quarto reading. Here the Folio goes wrong: 'Thorough tatter'd cloathes great Vices do appeare.' But this is cold-blooded perversion by somebody who thought he could improve the text. The meaning is that the smallest vices are seen (and punished) in the poor, but the privileged classes can conceal even the greatest.

Shakespeare seems to have preferred the spelling *totter'd* to 'tatter'd,' but both were used.

IV.vi.161. *Plate sin.* Theobald's excellent emendation for the Folio 'Place sinnes.'

IV.vi.170,171. *O matter . . . madness!* Much the same as Laertes' remark on Ophelia (*Hamlet* IV.i.178): 'A document in madness, thoughts and remembrance fitted.'

IV.vi.179. *block!* One of the remarkable topical anachronisms in the play. Lear (or Gloucester) is wearing one of the flamboyant hats that current fashion prescribed, either the 'copintank' or sugarloaf, or more probably one of the newer type with broad drooping brims. Lear suggests, there would be enough felt in a few of these to shoe a troop of horse, and this sets him off on a mad thought.

IV.vi.183. S.d. *three Gentlemen.* In the Folio text the frugality of the stage manager has reduced them to one.

IV.vi.188. *ransom.* He imagines himself on the battlefield and wounded.

IV.vi.191. *man of salt.* Even a man of salt, whose tears would not be good for the garden.

IV.vi.193. *Good sir.* This speech has had to be supplied from the second Quarto, but it is evident that something has dropped out of the first, which here assigns two consecutive speeches to Lear. In the extant copies of Q 1 no corrections have been noted in sheet I, which contains this part of the play, but, as Q 2 shows no other sign of independent authority, it looks as if it had been printed from a copy of Q 1 which did have this correction (P. A. Daniel).

IV.vi.209. *The main descry, etc.* We expect from hour to hour to get a view of the main body.

IV.vi.222. *To boot, and boot.* A quibble on the two senses of *boot,* one casual, the other spiritual. Gloucester offers Edgar his thanks, wishing him the bounty and benison of heaven *to boot* (in addition) and also, thinking of the deeper meaning, to his soul's *boot.* One might paraphrase thus: I give you hearty thanks; I invoke upon you the blessing of heaven also, and the latter (as my thanks are not) is a gift of real profit. The same pun is made, more jocosely, by Autolycus (*Winter's Tale* IV.iv.692f.): 'What an exchange had this been without *boot!* what a *boot* is here with this exchange!

IV.vi.231. *Chill not, etc.* Shakespeare makes Edgar use the South-western rustic dialect, which suits him as a Gloucestershire peasant and was familiar to the poet from childhood. It was sometimes called 'Cotswold speech' and became the usual mark of the stage countryman. It is characterized by retention of the old 'ich' for 'I' and the voicing (v, z) of the voiceless spirants, f and s.

IV.vi.236. *che vor ye.* See H. Kökeritz, "Elizabethan "che vore ye," "I warrant you," ' *Modern Language Notes,* February, 1942. Edgar's dialect may here be slightly wrong.

IV.vi.237. *batoon.* The older English form of French *baton.* The word made trouble. The Quarto printed it 'battero,' reduced in some copies to 'bat.' The Folio printed 'Ballow,' a word not otherwise known and probably, like 'battero,' a misreading of 'battoon.' Skeat and Mayhew (*Glossary of Tudor and Stuart Words*) suggest that a 'ballow' might be a quarter-staff made from 'ballow' wood, that is, wood with the bark removed, but this last sense also has very scanty support.

IV.vi.246. *British party.* In the army of the Britons (in opposition to the French). The Folio erroneously prints 'English.'

IV.vi.265. *and . . . tormenter.* One who torments herself with thoughts of you. The Quarto compositor set up what he thought he saw: 'and for you her owne for *Venter.*' The second Quarto and Folio omitted the words entirely (rather than print foolishness, presumably), but they are necessary. Goneril's conclusion is flat without them.

IV.vi.278. *fenced.* Here the Quarto keeps the Shakespearean word, the Folio 'seuer'd' (sever'd) being an easy but trite misreading. If Gloucester were distract, he would still have both thoughts and griefs, but they would be fenced or railed off from each other, so that, as he says in the next lines, the griefs (*woes*) would no longer be interpreted by thought and would lose the knowledge of themselves.

IV.vii. As Scene Third of this act is omitted in the Folio, Scenes Fourth, Fifth, and Sixth are naturally there marked 'tertia,' 'quarta,' and 'quinta,' respectively; but the present scene is marked 'septima,' as if there had been no omission. The Folio reduces this scene considerably and combines the Doctor and Gentleman in a single part.

IV.vii.9. *Yet . . . intent.* To be recognized now would limit the scope of my design.

IV.vii.16. *child-changed.* This means both 'changed into a child' and 'changed by the action of his children.'

IV.vii.30,31. *Was . . . winds?* The Quarto reading. The Folio has 'oppos'd' and 'jarring.' There is a reminiscence, as elsewhere in Shakespeare, of Marlowe's great line, 'Was this the face that launch'd a thousand ships?'

IV.vii.78. *cur'd*. Quarto reading. Folio, 'kill'd.' Here words of opposite sense give the same meaning and there is not a great deal to choose between them.

V.i.13. *as far . . . hers*. To the limit of what she has to give.

V.i.26. *Not bolds, etc*. A confused sentence. Albany apparently means: This business concerns me because France invades Britain, not because France countenances King Lear (in which support of Lear France is joined), with others whom, I fear, righteous and serious causes impel against us. The similarity in meaning as well as form between the two clauses beginning 'with others whom' (lines 22f. and 26f.) is very suspicious.

V.i.30,31. *For . . . here*. This is not the place to discuss these petty details of domestic friction. (For *particulars* in this sense, *cf*. I.iv.270.) The text is that of the Quarto as emended by Collier and Mitford: *poor* instead of 'dore.' The Folio reads 'For these domestic and particular broils Are not the question here,' which is easy but not very convincing. Shakespeare uses 'broils' to describe tumults of a more violent character than the bickerings Goneril wishes to suggest, and 'particular broils' is a muddy phrase not used elsewhere by Shakespeare. It took quite a number of people to make a broil. If the Folio text were original there would be no accounting for that of the Quarto; but if both rest on a manuscript in which the scribe had carelessly repeated the 'd' of *domestic* in the next word, making 'door' out of *poor*, the compositor or editor of the Folio may have felt justified in rewriting the line according to his own lights.

V.i.37. *riddle*. Since Goneril does not share her knowledge, the riddle remains obscure. This seems to be the meaning. There are two separate British armies which have entered the field successively: a Southern army, commanded by Regan and Edmund, and a Northern army commanded by Albany and Goneril. Regan most surprisingly invites her sister to join Edmund and herself in the Southern camp, and insists that she must come as chaperon (line 36). The 'riddle' Goneril reads is apparently Regan's secret intention to take advantage of her sister's visit to poison her. When we next see them, we find it is Goneril who has poisoned Regan. On the stage the words would be delivered with a sort of wink to the audience, inviting them to watch developments.

V.i.53. *By diligent discovery*. Edmund has been engaged on a reconnaissance. See IV.v.13,14.

V.ii.S.d. This, except the words, *and exeunt,* is the Quarto stage direction. The Folio version is drier and more technical.

V.ii.1. *bush*. The Folio makes it a 'Tree,' but a bush would be better cover for the old man in a battle.

V.ii.11. *Ripeness is all*. Compare *Hamlet* V.ii.225,226: '. . . if it be not now, yet it will come: the readiness is all' (Steevens).

V.iii.S.d. The Folio stage direction, probably composed by the stage-manager. Shakespeare may have written the simpler (and insufficient) version of the Quarto: *'Enter Edmund, with Lear and Cordelia prisoners.'*

V.iii.2. *their greater pleasures*. That is, the will of those personages of higher rank (than mine); *i.e.*, Goneril, Regan, and Albany.

V.iii.16,17. *And take upon's the mystery of things, As if we were God's spies*. Undertake to explain the mysterious ways of providence, as if we were spying on God Himself. This seems to be the only allusion in the play to the Christian God.

V.iii.18. *packs and sects of great ones*. Flocks and flocks of office-holders. The distinguishing thing about all these is that they have no personal existence, but are mere units in a transient crowd. The lowest ones are grouped in packs, like dogs or wolves; the most intelligent in sects, like philosophers.

V.iii.20. *Upon such sacrifices, etc*. A paganized echo of two well-known Scriptural passages: 'The sacrifice of God is a troubled spirit: a broken and contrite heart, O God, shalt thou not despise' (Psalm 51. 17), and 'for with such sacrifices God is well pleased' (Hebrews 13. 16).

V.iii.22,23. *He . . . foxes*. The last resort for getting foxes from their holes was fire. At Judgment Day the whole world will be subjected to the same treatment. Cordelia and Lear will dwell in their prison secure and united as foxes in their 'earths,' and nothing shall drive them hence but the angel of judgment with his fiery brand.

V.iii.24. *good years*. A vague phrase, perhaps Dutch in origin, suggesting some unnamed malign force. Still current in English dialect as 'The Goodgers.'

V.iii.33,34. *Thy . . . question*. The important service I am offering you cannot be discussed.

V.iii.39. *I cannot draw a cart nor eat dried oats.* I cannot live like a beast of burden: I must better my condition.

V.iii.40.S.d. As in the Folio, doubtless after the prompter's revision. Shakespeare's more casual way of dealing with such details probably appears in the Quarto version: '*Enter Duke, the two Ladies, and others.*'

V.iii.44. *I.* So the Folio, correctly. The Quarto, doubtless misled by the next line, has 'We.' Albany does not until much later (line 296 below) assume the royal 'We,' as Regan does in line 62. In line 45 *we . . . our* means 'all of us in our council' and 'our general safety.'

V.iii.57,58. *And the best quarrels in the heat are curs'd By those that feel their sharpness.* Edmund is saying that we are in no mood to judge dispassionately while suffering personal discomfort. He illustrates by a figure from an archery contest, *heat* meaning 'bout' (as in horse-races). A man who has been accidentally struck by one of the *quarrels* (cross-bow arrows) is more likely to curse it than to praise its extraordinary length of flight. Of course there is a quibble on the other sense of 'quarrel.'

V.iii.69. *your addition.* The title you have given him. The Quarto has 'your advancement,' probably a simplification of a rather unusual expression.

V.iii.71. *That were the most, if he should husband you.* The Quarto, followed by most editors, gives this speech to Goneril.

V.iii.77. The line is not in the Quarto, and the Folio reading, 'the walls is thine,' does not make sense. The conjecture, *whole,* is an old one, but anonymous.

V.iii.80. *The let-alone.* Waiver of one's claim, promise to pursue a *laissez-faire* policy; used of land with a clouded title. Goneril, Albany says, has no property in Edmund, no legal position in regard to him.

V.iii.82. The Quarto gives this line to Edmund, changing the words to 'prove my title good.'

V.iii.84. *attaint.* In conjunction with your attainder or accusation of dishonor. The Folio has 'in thy arrest' by influence of the line above.

V.iii.94. *mark.* The Folio reads 'make' and the Quarto 'prove' (probably repeated from line 92). In the Folio word the type is spread so as to suggest that an 'r' may have dropped out in printing.

V.iii.129. *Behold, it is the privilege of my tongue.* So the Quarto.

The Folio is confused here, missing both sense and rhythm: 'Behold it is my privilege, The privilege of mine Honours.'

V.iii.144. *What safe and nicely I might well delay.* For the sake of the record, Edmund makes the most of the fact that knights accepted challenges only from opponents of proper rank; but his action, like all his actions, is practical and self-interested. Deprived of military power, arrested as a traitor, and challenged by Albany, he has little to lose in encountering the unknown and a good deal perhaps to gain, since victory in trial by combat cleared the victor of the charges against him.

V.iii.146,147. *treasons, lie.* Accusations of treason and lying. *Which* in the next line refers to both.

V.iii.154,155. *Stop . . . stopple it.* Quarto reading. Folio: 'Shut . . . stop it.' It looks as if the Folio editor added the words 'Hold, sir' to complete his metrically deficient line, under the erroneous impression that line 156 is addressed to Edmund.

V.iii.160. *Ask . . . know.* Assigned to Edmund in the Folio.

V.iii.174. *I am here.* At the foot of Fortune's wheel, where his life began.

V.iii.183. *The bloody proclamation to escape.* In order to escape the hue and cry after me as a capital offender. When this sentence resumes after the parenthesis, the construction is altered. Instead of *taught me* in line 186, one would expect something like 'I was obliged.'

V.iii.205-207. *but another . . . extremity.* But if I were to recount another sorrow too fully, it would make much more (sorrow) and exceed the limit of endurance.

V.iii.209,210. *having . . . society.* When he had seen me as Poor Tom, he had shunned my abhorrent company.

V.iii.213. *threw him.* Threw himself. Theobald's emendation for the Quarto 'threw me.'

V.iii.222. *Alb. Speak, man.* The Quarto, omitting this short speech, throws the two questions of Edgar together and gives them as one speech to Albany.

V.iii.229. *Here comes Kent, sir.* The Quarto has this and the entrance of Kent follow the words 'Touches us not with pity' (line 232), which would seem to be more effective; but the metrical dove-tailing of speeches indicates that the Folio order was intentional.

V.iii.240. *Poison'd for my sake, and after slew herself.* A fine tumultuous line with a spondaic second foot. Read 'Poíson'd for mý sáke.'

V.iii.262. *Fall and cease!* Albany invokes the heaven and earth to display the accompaniments of Judgment Day. Fall, heavens! Cease, earth!

V.iii.274,275. *I have . . . skip.* Reminiscent of *Othello* V.ii. 261f.:

> I have seen the day
> That with this little arm and this good sword
> I have made my way through more impediments
> Than twenty times your stop.

V.iii.278,279. *If fortune . . . behold.* If the inconstant goddess can boast that she ever consistently loved one man and hated another, then one of those two (the latter) we behold. The meaning is clear if we understand the word 'respectively' before *lov'd.*

V.iii.288. *Nor . . . else.* Kent sees the grisly irony of Lear's words and puns on them: Neither I nor any of the rest of us have well come hither.

V.iii.294. *know our intent.* Albany, as the last survivor of those to whom Lear had transferred his absolute power, now assumes the royal prerogative and language in order to return to him what he had resigned.

V.iii.298. *You . . . rights.* That is, I wish you a happy return to the rightful dignities you have been deprived of.

V.iii.303. *my poor fool.* A phrase of tenderness, of course; but more telling if the rôles of Cordelia and the Fool were linked and Lear were felt by the audience to be taking leave of both of them. See note on III.vi.85.

V.iii.321. *Edg.* The Quarto gives this last speech to Albany, who might be expected to close the play, but the Folio is right. It is Edgar's reply to Albany's commission: *Rule in this realm.* Kent replies that he cannot serve because he expects to follow his master in death. Edgar replies that the young must accept the burden of the time and answer its demands by the dictates of their hearts rather than their heads: Speak what we feel, not what we ought (prudentially) to say. He accepts Albany's commission.

APPENDIX A

SOURCES OF THE PLAY

There are two tragic stories in this play: the sorrows of Lear and the subordinate tragedy of Gloucester. The former is one of the oldest and most familiar tales in English literature, given in its general outlines by many of the old chroniclers and romancers.[1] Raphael Holinshed, in his *Chronicles* (Chapters V. and VI. of the *Second Book of the History of England*, 2nd ed., 1587), has nearly all the main facts. He gives the names of the King, the three daughters, and their husbands; the answers of the three, saying how much they loved Lear, with Cordelia's consequent disgrace; the cruelty of the two dukes and duchesses to the King. But in his version, France defeats the two antagonists, restores Lear to the throne, and after his death, Cordelia becomes Queen. There was also an old play, entered in the Stationers' Register, 14 May 1594, *The moste famous Chronicle historye of Leire kinge of England and his Three Daughters*. On 8 May 1605, this quite un-Shakespearean and untragical piece was again

---

[1] See Wilfrid Perrett, *The Story of King Lear from Geoffrey of Monmouth to Shakespeare*, 1904. Shakespeare may be presumed to have known, besides Holinshed and the old play mentioned below, the version of John Higgins in *The Mirror for Magistrates* (1574). He appears to have taken the spelling of Cordelia's name and the manner of her death from Spenser's more succinct account (*Faery Queen*, 1590, Bk. ii. canto 10, st. 25–32). For a possible minor source see D. F. Atkinson, 'King Lear—Another Contemporary Account,' *E L H*, 1936, pp. 63–66.

entered on the Register as *The Tragecall historie of Kinge Leir and his Three Daughters, as it was latelie acted,* and printed in the same year. A number of minor similarities with Shakespeare's tragedy have been pointed out.[2]

The Gloucester story was taken from Sir Philip Sidney's *Arcadia,* 1590. In the second book, chapter 10, there is a narrative called *The pitifull state, and story of the Paphlagonian unkind king, and his kind son, first related by the son, then by the blind father.* This tale gives the essentials of the Gloucester-Edgar-Edmund plot, except as Shakespeare has interwoven them with the history of Lear and his three daughters.

The account of King Lear in Holinshed is brief enough to be quoted here in full, with no changes but in spelling:

'Leir the son of Baldud was admitted ruler over the Britons, in the year of the world 3105, at what time Joas reigned in Judah. This Leir was a prince of right noble demeanor, governing his land and subjects in great wealth. He made the town of Caerleir now called Leicester, which standeth upon the river of Sore. It is written that he had by his wife three daughters without other issue, whose names were Gonorilla, Regan, and Cordeilla, which daughters he greatly loved, but specially Cordeilla the youngest far above the two elder. When this Leir therefore was come to great years, & began to wax unwieldy through age, he thought to understand the affections of his daughters towards him, and prefer her whom he best loved to the succession over the kingdom.

'Whereupon he first asked Gonorilla the eldest, how well she loved him: who calling her gods to record, protested that she loved him more than her own life, which by right and reason should be most dear unto her. With which answer the father being well pleased, turned to the second, and demanded of her how well she loved him: who answered (confirming her sayings with great oaths) that she loved him more than tongue could express, and far above all other creatures of the world.

'Then called he his youngest daughter Cordeilla before him, and asked of her what account she made of him, unto whom she made this answer as followeth: Knowing the great love and fatherly zeal that you have always borne towards me, (for the which I may not answer you otherwise than I think, and as my conscience leadeth me) I protest unto you, that I have loved you ever, and will continually (while I live) love you as my natural father. And if you would more understand of the love that I bear you, ascertain [assure] your self, that so much as you have, so much you are worth, and so much I love you, and no more. The father being nothing content with this answer, married his two eldest daughters, the one unto Henninus, the duke of Cornwall, and the other unto Maglanus, the duke of Albania, betwixt whom he willed and ordained that his land should be divided after his death, and the one half thereof immediately should be assigned to them in hand: but for the third daughter Cordeilla he reserved nothing.

'Nevertheless it fortuned that one of the princes of Gallia (which now is called France) whose name was Aganippus, hearing of the beauty, womanhood, and good conditions of the said Cordeilla, desired to have her in marriage, and sent over to her father, requiring that he might have her to wife: to whom answer was made, that he might have his daughter, but as for any dower he could have none, for all was promised and assured to her other sisters already. Aganippus notwithstanding this answer of denial to receive any thing by way of dower with Cordeilla, took her to wife, only moved thereto (I say) for respect of her person and amiable virtues. This Aganippus was one of the twelve kings that ruled Gallia in those days, as in the British history it is recorded. But to proceed.

'After that Leir was fallen into age, the two dukes that had married his two eldest daughters, thinking it long yer [ere] the government of the land did come to their hands, arose against him in armor, and reft from him the governance of the land, upon conditions to be continued for term of life: by the which he was put to his portion, that is, to live after a rate assigned to him for the maintenance of his estate, which in process of time was diminished as well by Maglanus as by Henninus. But the greatest grief that Leir took, was to see the unkindness of his daughters, which seemed to think that all was too much which their father had, the same being never so little: in so much, that going from the one to the other, he was brought to that misery, that scarcely they would allow him one servant to wait upon him.

'In the end, such was the unkindness, or (as I may say) the unnaturalness which he found in his two daughters, notwithstanding their fair and pleasant words uttered in time past, that being constrained of necessity, he fled the land, and sailed into Gallia, there to seek some comfort of his youngest daughter Cordeilla whom before time he hated. The lady Cordeilla hearing that he was arrived in poor estate, she first sent to him privily a certain sum of money to apparel himself withal, and to retain a certain number of servants that might attend upon him in honorable wise, as appertained to the estate which he had borne: and then so accompanied, she appointed him to come to the court, which he did, and was so joyfully, honorably, and lovingly received, both by his son in law Aganippus, and also by his daughter Cordeilla, that his heart was greatly comforted: for he was no less honored, than if he had been king of the whole country himself.

'Now when he had informed his son in law and his daughter in what sort he had been used by his other daughters, Aganippus caused a mighty army to be put in a readiness, and likewise a great navy of ships to be rigged, to pass over into Britain with Leir his father in law, to see him again restored to his kingdom. It was accorded, that Cordeilla should also go with him to take possession of the land, the which he promised to leave unto her, as the rightful inheritor after his decease, notwithstanding any former grant made to her sisters or to their husbands in any manner of wise.

'Hereupon, when this army and navy of ships were ready, Leir and his daughter Cordeilla with her husband took the sea, and arriving in Britain, fought with their enemies, and discomfited them in battle, in the which Maglanus and Henninus were slain: and then was Leir restored to his kingdom, which he ruled after this by the space of two years, and then died, forty years after he first began to reign. His body was buried at Leicester in a vault under the channel of the river of Sore beneath the town.

'Cordeilla the youngest daughter of Leir was admitted Q[ueen] and supreme governess of Britain, in the year of the world 3155, before the building of Rome 54, Uziah then reigning in Judah, and Jeroboam over Israel. This

Cordeilla after her father's decease ruled the land of Britain right worthily during the space of five years, in which mean time her husband died, and then about the end of those five years, her two nephews Margan and Cunedag, sons to her aforesaid sisters, disdaining to be under the government of a woman, levied war against her, and destroyed a great part of the land, and finally took her prisoner, and laid her fast in ward, wherewith she took such grief, being a woman of a manly courage, and despairing to recover liberty, there she slew herself, when she had reigned (as before is mentioned) the term of five years.'

In the old play, Cornwall is the husband of Goneril, and appears in a somewhat better light than Regan's consort, the king of Cambria (Wales). But Shakespeare, as is hinted by the very first line of *King Lear*, deliberately made Goneril's husband a great and noble character, one of the finest gentlemen to be found among all his *dramatis personæ*; while Regan's husband has no redeeming features except energy and resolution. The Fool—one of the most remarkable among all Shakespeare's jesters—is another instance, if any were needed, of the dramatist's original creative power. Our respect for Shakespeare's genius is always heightened when we study his 'originals.' In this case, he took a melodramatic story with a 'happy ending,' and transformed it into a poignant tragedy, not merely of Lear, but of old age.

APPENDIX B

The History of the Play

The first performance of the play of which we have any record was (on the evidence of the Stationers' Register) in the presence of King James I at Whitehall Palace, 26 December 1606.[1] Lear is mentioned at the time of Burbage's death in 1619 as one of that actor's great parts, but the play, in its genuine form at least, had little popularity in the seventeenth century. Both the Jacobean contemporaneity of its social satire and its archaic, unclassical, and non-Christian setting would have alienated it from Restoration taste, though in 1662 there is an allusion to *King Lear* which seems to indicate that it was well known. In 1681 Nahum Tate made a revision which held the stage for a hundred and forty years, and was used by all the great eighteenth-century players. Edgar and Cordelia are united in marriage, and Kent and Lear live together. Tate's version seems insipid in comparison with Shakespeare's, but it was shaped to fit the fashion of the times, and this was the Lear that Garrick and Kemble played. Tate paid a compliment to Shakespeare in his Prologue:

> each Rustick knows
> 'Mongst plenteous Flow'rs a Garland to Compose,
> Which strung by his course Hand may fairer Show,
> But 'twas a Power Divine first made 'em Grow,

[1] For suggestions concerning the date of composition, which was probably during the preceding year, see notes on I.ii.106,109; III.iv.181; III.vii.71.

but his garland contained few of the original flowers, and the Fool was totally omitted.

It was in 1823 that the great actor Edmund Kean, who had often appeared in Tate's version, finally decided to return to the original text, saying to his wife, 'The London audience have no notion of what I can do until they see me over the dead body of Cordelia.' The effect was even greater than he had hoped for. W. C. Macready restored Shakespeare's text more fully, and was notably followed by Samuel Phelps, Henry Irving, and Tommaso Salvini, while the two most admired actresses of the century, Helen Faucit and Ellen Terry, made what they could of Cordelia's brief part. The most notable performances by American actors in the nineteenth century were by Edwin Forrest and Edwin Booth, who successively made an indelible impression on both critics and public. In the twentieth century, the play has been produced frequently in Germany and occasionally in Paris, but notable English performances have been few, while the best-known American production was long that of Robert Mantell, who deserved praise for giving his contemporaries their only opportunity to see the tragedy. Still, there is much truth in what Charles Lamb said over a century ago: 'The Lear of Shakespeare cannot be acted . . . the play is beyond all art.'

Index of Words Glossed

(Figures in full-faced type refer to page-numbers)

Index of Words Glossed 197

198 Index of Words Glossed

found: 11 (1.1.60)
frame of nature: 42 (1.4.274)
Fraretetto: 92 (3.6.6); 172
fraught: 40 (1.4.226)
from (away from): 53 (2.1.125)
from (contrary to): 58 (2.2.102)
front: 58 (2.2.112)
frontlet: 39 (1.4.193)
furnishings: 76 (3.1.29); 170

gad: 24 (1.2.26)
gale: 57 (2.2.82)
gall: 36 (1.4.118); 162
gallow: 79 (3.2.44)
garb: 58 (2.2.101)
gasted: 50 (2.1.56)
generation: 14 (1.1.118)
gentleness and course: 45 (1.4.348)
germens: 78 (3.2.8)
glass-gazing: 54 (2.2.18)
God's spies: 137 (5.3.17); 182
goest: 36 (1.4.125); 162
gone, sir: 118 (4.6.42)
good guard: 137 (5.3.1)
good years: 138 (5.3.24); 182
goodman: 56 (2.2.47)
gorgeous: 73 (2.4.269); 169
grac'd: 41 (1.4.251)
grace (majesty): 79 (3.2.40)
grace (mercy): 80 (3.2.59)
greater pleasures: 137 (5.3.2); 182
grossly: 22 (1.1.295)
guessingly: 98 (3.7.47)

had ... grace: 38 (1.4.170)
halcyon: 57 (2.2.81); 167
halters: 85 (3.4.53); 171
handy-dandy: 122 (4.6.149); 178
hard cure: 95 (3.6.102)
hatch: 94 (3.6.72)
hay ... sessa: 87 (3.4.98,99); 171
headier, more: 67 (2.4.110)
head-lugg'd: 107 (4.2.42)
heat: 139 (5.3.57); 183
heaven's benediction: 61 (2.2.165); 168
Hecate: 13 (1.1.111)
he's plain: 58 (2.2.104)
high-engender'd: 79 (3.2.23); 170
high noises: 96 (3.6.113)
hizzing: 92 (3.6.16)

holy cords ... too intrinse: 57 (2.2.77,78); 167
home: 82 (3.3.12)
hordocks: 112 (4.4.4)
house: 68 (2.4.153)
howe'er: 108 (4.2.66)
hundred: 94 (3.6.78)
hurricanoes: 78 (3.2.2)

idle (foolish): 31 (1.3.17)
idle (worthless): 112 (4.4.5)
I'll see that straight: 149 (5.3.285)
image: 148 (5.3.262)
image and horror: 29 (1.2.180)
immediacy: 139 (5.3.66)
impatience: 92 (3.6.5)
impertinency: 123 (4.6.170); 179
import: 114 (4.5.6)
important: 113 (4.4.26)
impress'd: 139 (5.3.51)
in: 73 (2.4.266)
in all: 89 (3.4.147)
in her hand: 136 (5.2. S. d.); 182
in the fleshment of: 59 (2.2.127)
in the least: 17 (1.1.194)
inflam'd respect: 20 (1.1.258)
ingenious: 127 (4.6.276)
innocent: 92 (3.6.7)
intelligent: 76 (3.1.25)
intelligent party: 91 (3.5.12)
intend: 19 (1.1.228)
interess'd: 13 (1.1.86)
interest: 11 (1.1.52)
interlude: 141 (5.3.90)
intrinse: 57 (2.2.78); 167
is it not well: 72 (2.4.239)
issue: 31 (1.4.3)
it: 40 (1.4.222); 163

jakes, a: 56 (2.2.69)
jealous: 135 (5.1.56)
jealous curiosity: 34 (1,4.70)
joint-stool: 93 (3.6.51); 173
Jug: 40 (1.4.230); 163

keep in-a-door: 36 (1.4.129)
kibes: 46 (1.5.9)
kindly: 46 (1.5.15)
kindness: 34 (1.4.61)
kite: 42 (1.4.268)
knapped: 67 (2.4.123)
knave: 10 (1.1.21)
knowledge and assurance: 77 (3.1.41)